AF332076

Murderous Hugs

Delphine Paquereau

MURDEROUS HUGS

Afterword by Dr Stéphanie Dauver

Max Milo Editions, Paris, 2023
www.maxmilo.com
ISBN : 978-2-315-01146-9

March 16, 1990

To the attention of Professor Alain[1], urologist at the University Hospital of Poitiers.

I was referred by the nephrologist, Dr. Brunet from La Rochelle. Delphine was operated in October 1987 for a bilateral reflux (according to Cohen's method) because she had urinary infections and fever repeatedly. She first had treatments for seven months without result, then the cysto showed a level four reflux, she had more infection. Very good on that side. She had a junctional problem that was operated on in September 1988. (The surgeon, Dr. Favre, is no longer in La Rochelle, for health reasons, he left).

Since January 1989, she started to have pain in her back again, always on the same side, which she made see on the left, she had treatments without result and the more time passed, the more she had pain.

When she pees, she has pain in her back upstairs.

She can hold it in, but it hurts her, it triggers big seizures, she needs to be given Spasfon.

---

1. All names in the text have been changed.

I am also called from school.

It was fifteen days on Sunday, she had 39° all night, no sore throat, no ear, no stomach, just her back. On Monday, the attending physician came, he could not touch her back, so she had six injections of Gentalline + Celestene, he sent me back to see the nephrologist Dr Brunet who found her tired, with dark circles on her eyes. He had a scintigraphy done in January 1990, I carried the photocopy that I was given.

So we were supposed to come and see you on March 28, 1990, but he brought the appointment forward. Because on his last IVU [intravenous urography, editor's note] he found the left pelvis dilated, on the scan slower on the left.

So he told me that he knows you very well and that you certainly need to reconnect and he prefers that you do it.

Dr. Brunet explained to me that it is better to operate now than to wait until her kidney is affected, and we can't leave her like that.

Ms. Robin.

FAMILY PORTRAITS

I would like to remember this story that I have kept in the back of my mind, but which occupies my mind and asks me many questions to which I have great difficulty in finding the answers. I think it would be useful to me. That's why I decided to reveal it, to remove this thick crust that prevents me from feeling good, confident, fulfilled, happy...

Mom and I always promised each other that we wouldn't talk about it anymore, that it was over. Except that after this promise, which I refused to betray, I had many bad moments to go through and I always came back to my mother to be reassured. I was always trying to find out why I felt so bad about myself, why the fear of dying invaded me again, as in childhood. I gradually became aware that this uneasiness probably came from the hospital wanderings I had experienced from a very young age, from the way my mother manipulated me, from all this sadness, these fears, all these emotions that had been so well repressed for years. My mind doesn't want to remember but my body hasn't forgotten anything and lets me know.

The need to understand where such discomfort came from occurred shortly before the birth of my first child, Lila.

In order to put things in order, to understand and to be able to take ownership of my story, I naturally felt the need to meet the doctors who had followed me as a child. Even if I didn't remember them, I wanted them to tell me how I was behaving, how mom was behaving, how they realized what was really going on, what they did to stop it... So I asked for copies of all my medical records from the different institutions I went to: CHU (university hospital center) of Nantes (hotel-Dieu and mother-child pavilion), CHU of Bordeaux, CH (hospital center) of La Rochelle, CH of Saintes, clinic of Niort, CHU of Poitiers, Necker hospital; as well as from my treating doctors, doctors Pelletier and Hacquin, from the judge of the children's court of Rochefort and the court of Marennes. There is only one file that I did not obtain, the one that should have been with our attending physician in Marennes and which seems to have been lost.

I also wanted to retrace my history from the beginning, that is, before I was even born, from the memories of what my mother told me during my childhood.

My mother is the last of her siblings. She was not a wanted child. Her own mother used to tell her that she was an "accident". Despite this, she has fond memories of her childhood. The siblings consisted of three sisters and two brothers. Girls and boys follow each other with perfect regularity and about ten years separate my mother from the eldest. They were all very close, they played and went out together. She sometimes tells me about the games and mischief she could do with them. I like to listen to her. I imagine her on roller skates with her brothers, sisters and girlfriends at the bottom of her building. She grew up in the Paris region, in a low-income housing project in Seine-Saint-Denis. Her mother was a janitor. Her father worked, I believe, in the municipal service of a neighboring town.

I remember my mother telling me about the love she received from her mother, her kindness, her gentleness, her hugs. She had her heart on her sleeve, she would tell me. I don't know what my mother's relationship was as a child with her father, but as an adult, she and he were close.

The whole family spent their vacations in Charente-Maritime. At first, my grandparents rented a house. Then they built their own in the region, with the aim of spending their retirement there. That's how my parents met. My father is originally from the town where my grandparents settled.

When their relationship became serious, my mother decided to quit her job and move in with my father, who didn't want to live near Paris. My mother's brothers and sisters stayed in the Paris area. We sometimes went there for the end of the year celebrations. My father would take us for a drive around Paris to see the illuminations. They were nothing like the ones back home, it looked great.

My father is also the youngest in his family. He has a sister and a brother. Son of a craftsman, he works as a boat mechanic in the family garage. Even if he never cut the link with his family, we are not very close to his family. My mother was not appreciated there, especially by my paternal grandmother. I think she didn't think she was good enough for her son. My parents had recurring financial worries. While my mother's parents were present and worked things out, my father's parents seemed to think that this was due to my mother's behavior. How my father felt about this estrangement, I don't know. I do know, however, that something happened that upset him.

His brother died in the 1990s. I have few memories of my uncle hanging himself on New Year's Eve. I know it was a hard time for Dad. Since Dad is a volunteer firefighter, his beeper went off and, despite the best efforts of his colleagues to spare him the sight of his brother hanging, he arrived at the scene of the tragedy, at the family garage. He was the one who took care of his brother. He never talked about it, I never saw him cry either. My mother said that my uncle did it because of a heartache.

My father's reaction to this tragedy sums him up: a kind and gentle person, but discreet and not very demonstrative of his emotions.

In my childhood memories, Dad is a cheerful and caring person. His hugs and kisses are very rare, but I never thought that he didn't love me. He never allowed me to doubt. When we spent time together, he was interested in all my childhood questions. And I asked a lot of questions, throwing "why? My father's patience is infinite; he tries to give an explanation to all my questions.

We are three children. I am the youngest and the only girl.

My mother often said that for the firstborn, she had no preference as to the sex. My father wanted a boy. However, for the second, she absolutely wanted a girl. Her wish seemed to be fulfilled two or three years later during the first ultrasounds, which delighted her.

But when she was born, she gave birth to a second boy in the nearest local hospital. She would later go on and on about how disappointed she was, even in front of my brother. I never knew how he felt about it, Paul never expressed what he thought.

So she asked for a third child, in the hope of having a daughter. My father accepted, to please his wife.

And eighteen months later, like in a fairy tale, the miracle happened: a girl, what a wonder!

Except that this marvel has started on a high note. Life already gave me my first test: I had to resist with all my strength to live. I was born with two turns of the umbilical cord around my neck, according to my mother. She is afraid to lose me, several doctors are working to free me from this cord that strangles me. And from my mother who is already holding me and suffocating me!

Mom loved to tell me how much she wanted a girl, how happy she was when I came into the world and how scared she was to lose me as soon as I was born. She would describe to me in great detail the scene of the doctors working around the bluish newborn, the doctors resuscitating the baby who was about to expire; she would tell me about it with such excitement that I wonder if she wasn't looking forward to this eventuality: losing me, the little girl she wanted so much.

So much wanted, really? Recently, someone around me told me that the reason we had a third child was because of the financial advantage it offered in terms of family allowances. This revelation upsets me, I don't know what to think about it. I always had in mind that Mom had wanted a daughter at all costs.

But is this closeness between the little girl and her mother really authentic? Is it me who, in the hope of keeping the image of a sincere love, voluntarily erased the inappropriate gestures and the hard words? The period of my 4-5 years old certainly contains our best moments. In my earliest memories, Mom and I are inseparable. We spend a lot of time together, I always follow her everywhere. She never complains about it, on the contrary, I think she is delighted.

"That's why I wanted a daughter, a daughter is always close to her mother, isn't that right my little Nénette?

To be close as my mother was with her own mother. As a child, I spent a lot of time with my grandparents. I would go with my mom. I remember that there were no games at their house. My brothers were bored and preferred to stay at home. I didn't care because the main thing was elsewhere, I was with my mother.

She did not work and was very available for us. She would pick us up at the kindergarten, prepare our snacks, stay with us on Wednesdays and during school vacations. Daddy had lunch with us every day, in spite of his work which took a lot of his time. As he was passionate about nature, we had a beautiful garden in which I spent a lot of time, between the swing and the pond full of fish. In the summer, Mom would take us to the beach and play with me in the waves. I have very happy images from that time.

However, before and after, things are much more ambivalent.

As I try to put myself in the shoes of this little girl, a memory comes back to me. We were spending a convivial moment at the home of a childhood friend of my father. In the hubbub of adult conversation, I hear my mother say:

"They're pissing us off these kids!"

The little girl in me is very sad to hear that. I am still sad today when I think about it.

Recently, I was told about a scene that really shook me up. I'm about two and a half years old. We are at a friend's house and I ask my mom to come and sit on her lap. I want a hug, kisses. My mother refuses, kisses her hand and puts it on my cheek. My insistence ends up annoying her, the caress becomes a "back and forth". This slap makes me feel a deep disarray today. It seems that my mother said at that time that Paul and I were not normal. Another "back and forth", terrible and unbearable this one, but which says a lot about our future family relations.

My older brother has been described to me as a rambunctious child. I believe it. Very early in my childhood, I didn't get along with him. He makes fun of me, he makes remarks about me because I am always stuck to my mother and I am always crying. It annoys him, he puts me down, and he gradually becomes an "accomplice" of my mother. It's like he's playing the role of Dad.

Things got worse when Mom started working. We got into the habit of staying home alone, my two brothers and me. I can't remember what the arguments were about, only the fear of being without mom, left to the "crazy" older brother. I would spend hours hiding in my room crying after a heated argument with him, or I would go out into the garden to hide in a shed that Dad had built for the pump of the water well in our house. Often he would end up riding his bike to a friend's house, and I would come home at that time.

Paul was also subjected to this tyranny. Their arguments were very violent. My brother was very nervous and would throw anything he could get his hands on anywhere in the house. He would punch the walls, the doors, and leave his mark. Hidden away, I would witness their scenes or hear their screams in the distance.

Although I love my younger brother, we communicate very little. We were unconsciously supportive but we could stay in the same room without talking to each other, and I had no desire to break the silence. Sometimes I felt sorry for the other. My mother's son, our eldest, whom I am unable to call "my brother," unaware of the harm he was doing, would sneer in a mocking tone.

I learned very quickly how to keep myself busy while waiting for mom to come back. I took care of the laundry, I tidied up, I cleaned the house. I was happy that mom wouldn't have to do it after her work. It also allowed me to think about something else and to contain the rage that the elder child was putting me in. I wanted to look strong in front of him and, above all, not to cry.

My hatred for him has grown over the years, to the point where it has become impossible for me to look at him. I systematically turn my head away so as not to see that ugly face. He disgusts me. He realizes it of course, it becomes his new game. When we are at the table, he eats next to me. I always end up getting up from the table and yelling all the insults that come to mind and lock myself in my room. The house is not very big, I hear my mother say to my father:

"No, but she's really not well! He didn't do anything wrong."

She speaks a little louder, knowing full well that I can hear her:

"You're not well, my poor girl! You need to get treatment!"

"Are you in pain, girl?"

"Complains of back pain, has repeated urinary tract infections."

I was 14 months old when my mother wrote this in my health book. A health book filled out more by her than by the doctors, which amazes me when I find out.

On another page of my health book, the one used by the doctor who performed the medical check-up in the kindergarten middle section class, I still recognize his handwriting: "Always complains of having a sore back (he says it's that she's growing up)."

To what extent was my so-called illness a well-thought-out plan by my mother from the very beginning? Did she already know how far she wanted to take us?

She would have liked me to be dependent on her for the rest of my life, to devote herself to her beloved and seriously ill child in order to gain the admiration of the doctors and those around us. To be the center of attention.

I don't remember exactly when it started, but I remember my mother asking me quite often if it burned when I peed, if my back hurt. So that I would know where my kidney was, she would press on it, it would tickle me, it was a very weird feeling. She took my temperature regularly and often took me to our doctor, Dr. Pelletier, who prescribed urine tests. I remember that to do them, my mother asked me to pee in a bowl, a bowl that we used for breakfast.

"It's okay, it washes out," she declared as she handed it to me.

So I complied, from the height of my 3 years, I went into the toilet and brought back the bowl filled with my urine. She was in charge of putting it in a tube with a big red cap, which we had gone to the laboratory to get. Before giving us the bottle, we were asked if it was for an ECBU (cyto-bacteriological examination of the urine). "Yes", my mother answered, holding out the doctor's prescription. We were told that we needed a sterile urine sample. But how could it be sterile after my mother's manipulation? The results were bound to be wrong, and no one would notice.

One day, in April 1987, when I was 4 years old, my mother told us that our maternal grandmother had died. She had been in the hospital for several weeks and my mother had been visiting her daily. She was in charge of the funeral arrangements. She had my grandmother's body brought back to her parents' house, displayed the coffin on the dining room table, and invited everyone who wanted to come and see her mother.

I didn't understand this adult ritual. Why didn't we spend this time as a family, in a small group? Why shout the event from the rooftops?

My mother thought I was unhappy because of my grandmother's absence. She regularly took me to her grave. I felt that she wanted me to be sad, so I was sad to please her. But I would have preferred not to go to the cemetery, I would have preferred to just think about her.

My mother wanted to cultivate the image of the best daughter a mother could have. And, by the same token, the best mother a daughter could have. Is that why, just two months after my grandmother's death, she regularly went back to the hospital, but this time with me?

June 1st, 1987
To the attention of Dr. Pelletier.

I have just seen in consultation the little Robin Delphine, 4 and a half years old, who presents a urinary incontinence day and night, with preserved micturition without anal sphincter disorders, but, according to her mother, associated with vaginal discharge (blood?).

The clinical examination of this child, whose physical and psychomotor development is quite normal, does not show anything particular (I even made her urinate in my office and she has a completely normal urination).

The intravenous urography and cystography that you had done showed nothing unusual. Indeed, there is no vesico-renal reflux or ectopic implantation of her ureters.

At first I reassured the mother and advised her not to dramatize this kind of problems which can reflect a psychological conflict with the family members. I advised her to give Ditropan, two tablets a day.

I will see little Delphine again in consultation after a month and a half of treatment and if her troubles persist, I will do a complete examination on the table and under general anaesthesia combining a urethrocystoscopy and a gynaecological examination.

Doctor Favre, surgeon, La Rochelle Hospital.

Our doctor finally decided to send me to see one of his colleagues to make sure I had kidney problems. Was this a real concern of the doctor or was it Mom's tenacity?

Dr. Pelletier had been my maternal grandmother's doctor. My mother had known him for a very long time and had a sympathetic relationship with him. A few weeks before my grandmother's death, perhaps he had wanted to spare my mother's concerns.

In any case, he should have been reassured by this advice from a specialist. My mother should have been reassured too and left me alone for the duration of my treatment. But only two weeks

"Are you in pain, girl?"

later, she brought me back for the tabletop examination that the surgeon had mentioned at the previous consultation. I have no recollection of this examination. But I do remember that all those appointments, which required me to get up early, made me tired, and that the different exams I had to take scared me.

June 15, 1987
To the attention of Dr. Pelletier, attending physician.

I therefore hospitalized for twenty-four hours the child Robin Delphine, 4 and a half years old, who presents daytime enuresis with the suspicion of metrorrhagia.

We therefore performed a complete examination under general anesthesia:

1) Dr. Leopold, a gynecologist, found nothing on gynecological examination.

2) As for me, I did not note anything at the urological examination apart from inflammatory lesions at the level of the urethra and the cervical region at the cystoscopy (attached the operative report).

It is therefore probably a case of bladder immaturity, and I would advise you to put her on Ditropan, two tablets a day, and an anti-infective treatment in a cyclic manner combining Nibiol for three weeks and then Iconcyl for three weeks.

I for one would love to see this child again in September.

Doctor Favre, surgeon, La Rochelle Hospital.

I have no recollection of whether or not I actually had urinary incontinence day and night, but I don't think I did. I also don't remember all the medications I was taking. I was intoxicated by them though!

Mom is convinced that there is something wrong with me. I let it happen. My mother seems to feel good, serene, when she is concerned about my health. She is full of attention and affection towards me in these moments. She reassures me with little words, calls me affectionately her Nénette, gives me her hand. Sometimes, I read sadness in her eyes; it worries me: if mom is sad, it means that it is serious what I have...

Finally, after two months, as nothing moved from Dr. Favre's side and my mother's concerns persisted, our attending physician advised her to go see another surgeon, at the Bordeaux University Hospital, for an additional opinion.

"It's better to have several opinions than one," I would often hear my mother say, no doubt to justify the multiple consultations she requested from many doctors. I think she was mostly waiting to find the one who would confirm that her daughter was indeed sick and required endless surgery and care.

She took me to Professor Verneuil, a pediatric surgeon. I remember that we had driven a long way by ambulance to meet him; by ambulance, yes, because my mother did not take the car to my consultations, but systematically called an ambulance driver, always the same one. She claimed that the car was too expensive. But this allowed her to be noticed and to formalize my status as a seriously ill child who required specific attention, which she wanted to reap. I was uncomfortable with this vehicle parked in front of our house. What would the neighbors think?

Before meeting the doctor, my mother recommends that I tell him where I am suffering and, while talking, she pats me hard on the back to make me feel the pain where my kidney was located.

"Don't forget to wince when he checks you, so he can see that you're in pain."

Professor Verneuil was a tall, mustachioed man who spoke mainly to me, asking me directly about my condition. I obeyed Mom's instructions, certain that she was right: if I didn't help the doctors, how would they find out what I was suffering from?

"Are you in pain, girl?"

From opinion to opinion, from doctor to surgeon, from treatment to treatment, my mother drags her little girl behind her, eager to convince the specialists of my ills. Little by little, she succeeded.

I have just seen little Robin Delphine in consultation and she continues to have recurrent urinary tract infections.

As you know, I asked for a retrograde cystography for control. This examination found a stage III active (?) left vesico-renal reflux.

Given the recurrent infections despite treatment and the importance of the reflux, surgical treatment is necessary.

Little Delphine will be hospitalized in surgery starting Thursday, October 1 and I will operate on Friday, October 2.

In addition, I had a new check-up pelvic ultrasound done, which was completely normal.

In the meantime, I asked the mom to put her on Nibiol.

Doctor Favre, surgeon, La Rochelle Hospital.

When I read this letter today, I wonder: three months earlier, all the clinical examinations were perfect and suddenly, a surgical intervention is necessary! Wouldn't my mother have been a bit insistent? Would the surgeon have been convinced of a real need for surgery? I know that she invoked the repeated urinary tract infections at every turn, presenting the results of the ECBU, the reliability of which I doubt, given the conditions in which I carried them out. Indeed, my mother must have known that not collecting the urine in sterile tubes distorted the analyses.

For the second time in less than four months, I am hospitalized.

In the ambulance that takes us to Bordeaux, I am afraid. My stomach hurts, I wonder what will be done to me, what will happen. My mother seems to be serene, she is talking with the ambulance driver she knows well, since she also went to the hospital with him for my grandmother.

In this hospital, I feel lost; the staff doesn't talk to me much, the establishment is old and ugly. They put me on a stretcher to take

"Are you in pain, girl?"

me to the operating room, they cover me well because I have to go through the courtyard. It was cold. I was left alone in a cubicle where I had to wait. I shivered, I was cold and scared, I wanted my mother to be with me. In the operating room where I was finally taken, I was still as cold as ever. There is a big light just above me that makes me turn my head. I am covered with warm sheets because I am shaking so much. Despite everything, I open my eyes wide, I want to see everything, to observe what they all do. I don't want to relax, I don't want to be put to sleep. I won't see anything. What if I don't wake up? What if I'm allergic to the anesthetic, that my heart can't take it? I won't see my mom or dad or my brothers again, like in the movies Will they be sad? I don't want to die, I want to get better, I want to go back to school, I think of my kindergarten friends who don't have any health problems, they have fun, they learn, they play I'm here, in the cold, in the middle of the gowns and the naked lights, on this table.

The staff prepares the infusion, they prick me, they put a mask over my nose, they ask me to count. I can't fight it, nothing and no one will make the operation be cancelled. I fall asleep, I feel discreet tears running down my cheeks. They will see that I don't feel well, they will postpone the operation...

When I wake up, what a relief! I am still alive, everything went well, and maybe I am cured for good now! I stay a few days in Bordeaux, I am alone. My mom calls every day, I'm happy to be able to talk to her and to hear her, I can't wait for her to come and get me, I miss her.

When I finally come home, she is very attentive to me. Dad, on the other hand, shows me the same affection as he does my brothers, no more. I start to wonder about my mother's behavior. Maybe she is too protective? At the same time, that means she cares about me, doesn't it? Are my brothers jealous of my mother's attention to me?

I will see Dr. Favre again for follow-up examinations a month and a half after the operation.

March 22, 1988

To the attention of Dr. Pelletier, attending physician.

I am sending you the result of the radiological control of the little Delphine Robin with delay because I have only just received it, please excuse me.

Urethrocystography shows satisfactory bladder replenishment, without active or passive vesico-ureteral reflux.

Intravenous urography is functionally and morphologically normal.

Doctor Favre, surgeon, La Rochelle Hospital.

An ambivalent mother

We are in September 1988. I am starting kindergarten.

I think I'm just like the other kids: I go to school every day, I play with friends on Saturdays... The only tests my mom asks me to do are the ECBU, which is done at home, and blood tests that we go to the lab for before school or that a nurse comes to do at home. Nothing too restrictive for the little girl that I am, and it's even a little respite after the many trips to the surgeons and the heavy exams I've had.

What's getting annoying, and increasingly bizarre for me, is that Mom keeps asking me the same questions regularly:

"Does it burn when you pee? Does your back hurt?"

While asking me the question, she presses where she thinks the kidney is. Maybe she is not mistaken, that the kidney is located where she presses her fingers, because indeed I feel a little discomfort under the pressure of her hand. I can't figure out if it really hurts.

She takes my temperature often, considers it useful to call Dr. Pelletier, and would like him to come at once. Faced with his immediate unavailability, which annoys her and which she blames on the doctor's poor organization, she invokes an emergency, and invents a fever that I don't have.

"Why are you lying?" I ask her when she hangs up.

"To get him here faster. Otherwise, it won't be here until tomorrow or the day after."

In my childish mind, I know something is wrong: the temperature is not too high, so I'm fine, right? So why does she tell the doctor that he has to come quickly? Am I sick or not? I can't figure out how I feel, whether I have something or not. So I give in to my mother's devotion and attentions. I lie on the couch under a comforter, I am not allowed to go and play in my room, I have to stay still until the doctor comes, even if I don't feel any pain, even if I want to get up. Mom pampers me, puts on the television for me. I don't like missing school to wait for the doctor, but I like this time alone with my mom.

When the doctor enters, I recognize the smell of his cigarette mixed with his perfume, it raises my heart every time. In spite of her concern, my mother doesn't feel any confusion to give him all the important information about my condition: pain, temperature, vomiting... He checks me, hardly asks me any questions. Anyway, I understood that no matter what he says, it will never suit my mother; after he leaves, she will ask me the same questions.

She seems to be more and more concerned about my health, it worries me that she is so worried when I feel fine. But I understand, she loves me so much that she wants to make sure I'm doing well. Dad doesn't seem to be anxious. He eats lunch with us and goes back to work as usual when I'm cooped up at home. Mom and I sit on the couch, she takes some medicine to calm her growing anxieties. We snuggle up together and watch the afternoon soap operas in which children often die. Mom doesn't seem to be affected by these tragic stories. I am terribly saddened by them. I don't want my health concerns to be serious or to die.

The more the days and weeks go by, the more I get fed up. Yet, I love the attention she gives me, that she cares about me. That means she loves me, doesn't it? But I would like her love without all these tests, without these doctors around us. When I'm lying in bed like a sick person, I would like her to just hold me, without asking me all her questions and without feeling me up.

I sometimes doubt her affection. Maybe she just likes me to be sick, not the little girl? Why do I often feel lonely and unhappy?

When someone or something makes her angry, my mother seems to forget about my brothers, my father and me. I feel abandoned. She is in a state of excitement that makes her hateful, she no longer cares about the house. Despite the anger I feel towards her in these moments, I want to help her, perhaps in the hope of attracting her goodwill. I make the beds, dust, vacuum, clear the table. I feel deeply unhappy, I take myself to hate this life, I hide behind the house, where my brothers can't find me, and I cry. I would like to grow up quickly, to leave this home.

I pretend that everything is fine though, I am nice to her, I need her love, that she shows me a gesture of affection, that she pays attention to me, like when she thinks I am sick.

"Are you okay, Mom?

- Don't bother, it's grown up stuff, what do you care?"

I am furious, I would like to insult her too, I find her ugly when she is in this state. The expression on her face is hard, I don't recognize her anymore.

My father escaped this difficult atmosphere by working a lot, spending time at the fire station where he was a volunteer and going out with his colleagues. The eldest, a budding tyrant, takes advantage of this to exercise his authority and push Paul and me to the limit. He knows that our mother will not pay any attention to his actions, or even that she will support him. When I run away to my room to cry, I always hope that she will react, take my defense. But she throws me, like a slap that burns me:

"Cry, you'll pee less."

Is it like this in other families? Did the other children get a hug or a story before going to sleep? Once we were in bed, the threat of the whip hung over our heads if we talked, played, or got up.

I suffer from her behaviors, the fear of abandonment inhabits me, perhaps it is also for that that I enter in her game of the sick child, it is the only argument that I have to maintain her near me, to arouse her interest. She doesn't give any respite to the little girl that I am, in spite of Dr. Favre's last examination report, which should have made her stop any further investigations and rejoice at my "good health". And even worse...

February 22, 1989
To the attention of Dr. Pelletier, attending physician.

I see Delphine Robin again in consultation today, whom I had not seen since September 1987. It seems that the treatment of the bladder immaturity was effective since she now has no more diurnal or nocturnal leaks, and the cystography performed shows no signs of bladder immaturity with a bladder of good capacity.

As for her reflux, which was operated on, there does not seem to be any recurrence that could explain this child's UTI problem.

So I think there is only one abnormality that can be noted, a small grade I pyeloureteral junction on both sides that I don't think is involved in these UTIs. However, if this child continued to have significant infections, it might be advisable to do a kidney scan with a Lasilix excretion test to see if the emptying slope of this kidney is normal or not.

On the other hand, I don't see any obvious etiology for the urinary tract infections that this child has and I think that if she has any recurrence of hyperthermia with posterior pain, it would be advisable to put her on parenteral antibiotics to clean her kidneys properly.

On the other hand, the mother tells me that she has discovered a small swelling in the middle of the back of the chin at the base of the tongue which probably corresponds to a cyst of the thyroglossal duct. As I explained to her, these cysts have no spontaneous tendency to regress and always end up getting infected sooner or later. So I think it's best to plan to have them surgically removed before any infection occurs. In fact, superinfection poses major technical problems for us because we have to dissect this cyst to the base of the tongue by removing the anterior arch of the hyoid bone if we want to avoid recurrences.

Professor Verneuil, surgeon, Bordeaux University Hospital.

"Mom is happy, an operation is coming up!"

That's really how I feel at the time, "Mom is happy!" I look at her, her eyes are shining, she seems really pleased with the news, she is full of excitement, impatience.

Before leaving for the hospital, she carefully prepares my luggage, as if I were going on a trip for ten or fifteen days. She puts a bottle of cologne in the toiletry bag. I hate it, for me it's an old man's thing. But I don't tell her, she seems to like it so much. I also hate the basket she fills with food and drinks, like we're going on a picnic with 15 people. It seems completely out of proportion to me.

Before going into surgery, I still have to go through a whole series of tests. I remember one in particular, which I didn't like at all and which made me terribly uncomfortable. It was a retrograde cystogram, I think.

I am lying naked, a tube is passed through my urethra, I have to drink a large quantity of water and, while the doctor is taking the pictures, a kind of balloon is placed on my belly that is squeezed very hard and I am asked to pee. The urine came out of the tube, I was deprived of all my privacy, I felt humiliated. Inside me, I yell for them to leave me alone, but no one sees my anger, I hold it all in, I remain the obedient child who wisely undergoes everything that is inflicted on her, without knowing if it is justified or not. The hospital staff compliments me on my patience, my courage. I am annoyed, everyone talks to me as if I were a baby, but once again I refuse, I only answer with a shy, polite smile. All these constraints

An ambivalent mother

are imposed on me and I let them do it without saying anything, because my mother loves me, she wants the best for me and, above all, to find out what is wrong with me!

All this to confirm that there is nothing abnormal.

The surgeon only put me on antibiotics "to clean the kidneys".

As for the swelling under the jaw, discovered by Mom, a pathological analysis performed after the operation revealed a histologically normal lymph node.

Today, I have the feeling that the attending physician could have reasoned with my mother so that she would stop going from hospital to hospital, from surgeon to surgeon, inflicting me with all these examinations and almost useless operations. The letters from all the doctors are however clear: this little girl is fine, she says nothing, it is the mother who speaks, it is she who is determined.

The little girl realizes deep down that this surgeon in Bordeaux, Professor Verneuil, is beginning to doubt the symptoms announced by Mom. But does he think that it is the child or the mother who is lying? And why doesn't he do anything to stop this delirium?

"It's for Your Own Good"

May 2, 1989
To the attention of Dr. Pelletier, attending physician.

You will find enclosed the operative report of your patient Delphine Robin to whom I performed her endoscopy this morning.
I think her pain and hematuria are due to flare-ups of hematuric cystitis, so I put her on medication for a month.
Next consultation in one month.

Professor Verneuil, surgeon, Bordeaux University Hospital.

May 17, 1989
To the attention of Dr. Pelletier, attending physician.

Thank you for doing a DTPA scan with a Lasix test on little Delphine.
This young girl had a uretero-vesical reimplantation two years ago.
She may currently have left lower ureteral stenosis.
This stenosis would be only partial and would lead to painful phenomena with hyperdiuresis.

So I would like to know with the elimination slope of Lasilix whether or not there is an obstruction on his urinary tract.

Professor Verneuil, surgeon, Bordeaux University Hospital.

Here is the surgeon from Bordeaux who is going to perform an operation on my left kidney, the same as the one already performed by the surgeon from La Rochelle, Dr. Favre, two years before.

Again the preparations for the hospital, the satisfaction of my mother, the compassion of the nurses, which annoys me, the distress which chokes me.

June 13, 1989
To the attention of Dr. Pelletier, attending physician.

You will find attached the operative report of your patient Delphine Robin.

I operated on her Cohen type vesico-ureteral reimplantation dysfunction this morning.

It seems that her left ureter suffered during the first operation, which could explain the functional disorders presented by this child.

I plan to keep it, in principle, seven days.

She will leave with a triple alternating antibiotic treatment and I entrust you to check the sterility of her urine by monthly ECBU.

I will see her in consultation in one month for a urography and in three months for a cystography.

Professor Verneuil, surgeon, Bordeaux University Hospital.

September 6, 1989
To the attention of Dr. Pelletier, attending physician.

I saw Delphine Robin again today, who continued to have pain in her left flank, which was permanent without improvement.
I think that despite the urographic aspect, we can evoke the responsibility of her left pyeloureteral junction syndrome and, in agreement with her mother, I will operate on Thursday September 14.

Professor Verneuil, surgeon, Bordeaux University Hospital.

September 14, 1989
To the attention of Dr. Pelletier, attending physician.

You will find attached the operative report of your patient, Delphine Robin.
I operated on her left pyelo-ureteral junction stenosis this morning.
I plan to keep her for seven days. She will leave with a triple antibiotic treatment alternating for a month. I will see her again in a month for an IVU.

Professor Verneuil, surgeon, Bordeaux University Hospital.

These hospitalizations are difficult. My mother can't stay with me during all my stays, she has to take care of the others at home. I feel neglected.

"It's for your own good," she says to me every time.

I don't remember a visit from my father. He let my mother handle the situation completely, he trusted her completely, not doubting that his daughter was indeed sick.

I do remember an uncle and an aunt on my maternal grandfather's side who sometimes came in the afternoons. It made me feel good, I thought they must have loved me very much to come and visit me like that.

After this operation, my mother continues to talk about pain in her left kidney. I'm starting to get tired of it. Sometimes I complain to my mother.

"I'm tired of going to the hospital, tired of the tests, tired of the operations.

- And aren't you tired of having kidney pain? If you want all this to stop, you have to tell the surgeon that you are really in pain, even if you exaggerate a little, at least he will understand. And make a face so he can see that this is not a show. This is all for your own good."

I would just like to continue going to school regularly. I started first grade at my local school with Mr. Pic, a great teacher who I love, kind, caring and patient. I don't work very well, but I like what I learn and the company of my classmates. I have found all the people I was with in kindergarten and have made good friends with them. Despite my lack of self-confidence and even if I don't dare to impose myself in the group, I have the impression that they accept me well. I forget about my health worries and the tumultuous atmosphere at home with the oldest member of the family when I am there. But I miss school too much, it makes me sad.

My relationship with my mother intensifies again during this time; I sometimes feel like she's abandoning my brothers for me. But maybe it's just that they are growing up and don't need her as much?

Between the various check-ups, Mom continues to press on my kidney, creating a pain that I would not experience if she left me alone, but which allows her to give reason to all the medical investigations that she demands and that I accept out of love for her.

"Are you in pain?"

Sometimes I shrug my shoulders so as not to answer that age-old question that I can't stand. I know she wants me to say "yes", that my "no" might disappoint her and she might not pay as much attention to me anymore.

During the follow-up consultation, one month after my last operation, Professor Verneuil stood up to me and explained that these pains could be psychological. I don't know exactly what this word means, but I understand that he thinks I am lying to him. This makes me feel uncomfortable and annoyed, I don't want him to think I'm faking it. I would like to explain to him that it is not me who lies, that it is mom who exaggerates a little on the pains, on the blood that I never saw, on the temperature... But she would be furious.

My mother is starting to dislike Professor Verneuil, she talks about it with our ambulance driver on the way home, the one I like best, the one that brings us home.

Professor Verneuil wrote a letter about this check-up to our other doctor, Dr. Hacquin, who arrived in our commune in 1989 and who is the fire department doctor. When Dr. Pelletier didn't arrive quickly enough for my mother's taste, she called him, having met him through my father. But I know that he annoys her a bit, with his baba cool attitude and his slightly cynical humour. She feels that he takes my health lightly, that he is nice, but not very competent.

I see Delphine Robin again today, on September 14, 1989. This child still has her painful problems.

So I presented his case to Professor Lelièvre, who is our nephro-logist, to see if there might be an underlying disease that I would have missed until now. Mr. Lelièvre remains very dubious about an underlying nephropathy problem insofar as there is no proteinuria and no sign of nephrosis so far. Secondly, if it was acute glomeru-lonephritis pain, it only persists for two or three weeks and then disappears completely; and in any case, the biological signs would have told us this diagnosis.

So there is another possibility, which is that this child has small hemorrhages in her kidney and that these pains are due to renal colic from migration of small clots that may result either from Berger's disease, which is an IGA deficiency, or perhaps from a vascular spot on one of the renal cavities that we have not been able to demonstrate up to now, either by IVUS or by the procedure that I had performed.

I therefore think that it would be advisable for you to have him perform two additional examinations: on the one hand, an IGA blood test, which, if normal, would enable us to rule out the diagnosis of Berger's disease, and on the other hand, observation of the red blood cells contained in the urine under a phase microscope to see whether or not there are crenellated red blood cells. Indeed, it is known that hematuria of renal origin give crenellated red blood cells and that hematuria of low origin give perfectly round hematuria [...].

However, I will put Delphine on anti-inflammatory drugs in addition to the treatment you have started in order to try to calm her pain, some of which may be inflammatory in origin. As soon as you have been able to have these tests done, I would be grateful if you could keep me informed, so that we can decide on the best course of action for this child in the coming weeks. In the meantime, of course, the treatment you have prescribed should be continued if you think it is useful.

Professor Verneuil, surgeon, Bordeaux University Hospital.

So here I am again, undergoing examinations, this time a scanner. This one bothers me a little less than the others. I don't have to show up naked, just in my panties, and even though the infusion is painful, I'm used to it. I try to respect it to the letter, otherwise I have to start again and I really don't want to. I must not move, not even breathe for a few seconds. A product circulates in the pipe, which first heats my throat and then my whole body. It only lasts a few seconds, but the sensation is very strange and quite unpleasant. And then, of course, my mom doesn't stay close to me: it's a dangerous exam, you shouldn't be exposed to it for too long. However, I often take these exams.

With the radiological results in hand, we return to see Professor Verneuil.

October 31, 1989
To the attention of Dr. Hacquin, attending physician.

So I saw the CT scan and little Delphine Robin. I think there may be a small renal angioma that can cause these hemorrhages with renal colic.
I therefore put her on antihemorrhagic and antispasmodic treatment for two weeks. If this treatment was not effective, I would make an appointment for a digital angiography and to consider a possible surgical removal.
Good luck!

Professor Verneuil.

Probably because Mom didn't like it when Professor Verneuil started to question the validity of our complaints about my kidney, we went to a third surgeon.

FAKE BACKGROUND AND PUNCHES

I don't remember Professor Rodier at all. It is by going through my medical files in detail that I discovered his name and the establishment to which he was attached: the Necker-Enfants malades hospital. I even consulted in Paris! It must have been during a stay at a maternal uncle's house for the end of the year holidays.

I phoned the Necker secretariat to check that I had a file with them. About two months later, I received a copy.

Since I don't remember this hospital at all, I think I only went there for a consultation. But to my great surprise, I was hospitalized there and underwent a whole "battery" of tests, the same as usual, as well as a small operation.

I cry, I think of the little girl I once was, so she's been through this again. What stuns me is that I don't remember. I was six and a half years old, and I remember my other exams and surgeries from that time. I try to concentrate to remember even one image of this new hospital wandering. But nothing, nothing at all, I only remember this little girl in the hospital in Bordeaux, the operating room, her solitude in her room...

I also realize that I wasn't crying. If a few tears escaped, they would run down my cheeks discreetly. Today, the adult that I am cries like a child, I can't help it, I don't want to help it. I accept and understand that the little girl is sad. I remember at the time, I was congratulated:

"What a brave little girl! That's good, Delphine."

I responded with a sympathetic smile.

December 28, 1989
To the attention of Dr. Pelletier, attending physician.

Delphine has two brothers, aged 10 and 8, with no particular problems. The mother is being followed for an anomaly of the right pyeloureteral junction, but has not been operated.

Delphine presented urinary tract infections quite early in life, associated with a picture evoking bladder immaturity. This situation led to a surgical intervention in October 1987 to treat bilateral vesico-renal reflux. She was operated on by Dr. Favre in La Rochelle who performed a bilateral Cohen procedure on October 2, 1987. The postoperative course was simple until April 1989: she then presented pain in the left lumbar fossa, which led to a consultation in Bordeaux with Dr. Verneuil, who performed an IVU, cystography and scintigraphy, leading him to conclude that there was a dysfunction of the left Cohen and to reintervene on June 13, 1989.

After this operation, because of the persistence of pain and because of the slightly chubby aspect of the left pyelo, a resection of the left pyeloureteral junction was performed on September 17, 1989. Since this operation, the child presents persistent pains: they can occur at any time during the day, generally completely isolated, without nausea, without vomiting, leading to a small decrease in appetite. No particular mictional disorder. No digestive disorders. No diarrhea, the child has a bowel movement every day. I specify that the child does not cough.

In view of the persistence of these pains, which were extremely precise for the child, in the left costo-vertebral angle, a CT scan was performed on October 26, 1989 and an angiography on November

20, 1989: these two examinations appeared to be strictly normal. The only particular point is that the ECBU of December 15, 18 and 19, 1989 showed the persistence of red blood cells. I think that recent urological interventions can be mentioned to explain this microscopic hematuria.

I examined Delphine very carefully: the examination can be considered as strictly normal. The examination included: an abdominal examination, a cardiological, pulmonary, neurological examination, an examination of the lymph nodes.

BP 13/8 - tension a little high maybe due to emotion.

In total:

I can't give a precise explanation for Delphine's pain.

I believe that we can, however, affirm that there is nothing serious given the clinical examination and the radiological examinations (scanner and angio) presented to me by this family.

For my part, I will stop worrying and stop giving painkillers; in fact, the mother gives Spasfon and Baralgine tablets quite regularly. We must be wary of a possible hematological impact of these medications.

As for me, I will have a count done in two months with a cyto-bacteriological examination of the urine.

Professor Rodier, Necker-Enfants malades hospital.

So there is nothing... But then why does everything continue?

My mother hits my left kidney harder and harder when she examines me at home, before each new consultation. Each time we are alone in the living room with the eldest. I hate him, he's a scumbag, but I don't tell Mom, they're very close and they get along very well when they say mean things to me. They obviously pick times when Paul and my dad are out. I know that what is happening is not normal and that my mother and her son would not like me to talk about it, and even less to the doctors. And I accept this game of silence, terrorized by the elder and wanting to protect my mother from the suspicious eyes of the doctors. I don't want them to think she's a bad mother, or that she's abandoning me.

She is sitting on the couch, legs spread, I am standing in front of her, from behind, she is punching me in the left side, I am holding back my tears, I want to be strong against them.

"But why are you doing this to me?

- This is to make sure that you know where it hurts once we get to the consultation. That way, the doctor can see that you're really in pain, and he can believe you and do the right thing for your kidney. And don't pee, so the doctor can see that something is wrong.

She shows no compassion for the sadness I have to show. Her eldest son sneers like a moron. Once he wanted to hit my kidney, but I didn't let him, I feel he is dangerous. I ran around the dining room table to get away from him, I got on all fours to get under it, I screamed. My mother did not help me, she did not react.

At the hospital in La Rochelle where we return, we meet Dr. Brunet, nephrologist, who refers us to Dr. Lemoine, urological surgeon.

February 2, 1990
To the attention of Dr. Lemoine, urologist.

You will soon be seeing 7-year-old Delphine Robin, who has a complex urological problem.

Her personal history includes an appendectomy that was performed on October 10, 1986. In October 1987, she was operated on in La Rochelle by Dr. Favre for bilateral reflux. In the following two years, lumbar pain on the left side reappeared and the anti-reflux device was used again on the left side in June 1989 by Dr. Verneuil, in the department of Professor Bonneau in Bordeaux. Unfortunately, the painful symptomatology persisted in the absence of any urinary tract infection and, in September 1989, this child was operated on for a junction syndrome, again on the left side. All these operations were accompanied by scans which showed before and after the operation a delay of evacuation on the left side. Delphine also had a CT scan which did not bring any additional element to the diagnosis.

Currently, this child still complains of left-sided back pain that is independent of any urination but requires her to urinate. There is no fever or urinary tract infection, and apparently renal function remains normal.

I think that the problem must be taken up again in its entirety because one cannot eliminate a passive reflux always on the left or possibly a stenotic recurrence at the level of the junction on the left.

It should be noted that the mother of this child would be a carrier of a right junction syndrome, that the maternal aunt would also present a junction syndrome and that the grandmother of this child would have died of a uraemia crisis in December 1987 at the Richelieu clinic in Saintes.

On examination, I did not find anything very special apart from pain on palpation of the left hypochondrium and left lumbar fossa. Her weight is 19 kg for a height of 117 cm, which is within normal limits.

The mother is of course warned of a possible re-intervention.

Doctor Brunet, nephrologist, La Rochelle Hospital.

Of course my mother is warned about a possible re-intervention, since that is what she wants more than anything else and she is ruthlessly determined to achieve it.

Including lying about family history and dates of events.

My grandmother did not die of uraemia but of bowel cancer at the hospital in Saintes in April 1987. On the other hand, I am not sure that my aunt is a carrier of a junction syndrome, since my mother had explained to me once that she had four kidneys, two on each side, the extra kidneys being non-functional and hooked to the other two. How do I know what the truth is? Similarly for my mother, I don't remember hearing her say that she also had junction syndrome.

But her assertions allow her to support her diagnosis in front of doctors who cannot verify what she says and who see nothing in the clinical examination concerning me.

February 6, 1990

To the attention of Dr. Pelletier, attending physician, copy to Dr. Brunet, nephrologist, CHU La Rochelle.

I was brought to see your patient, the child Robin Delphine, 7 and a half years old, in consultation today, at the request of Dr. Brunet, for her problems of lumbar and left flank pain.

This child, who has a long history of surgery and radiological investigations, complains, according to her mother, of pain lateralized to the left, linked to a state of bladder repletion obliging her to urinate frequently and complicated, on the occasion of two recent episodes, by incontinence.

On the other hand, no infectious complication has been noted since the last operation in September 1989.

In view of the radiographic findings in my possession, I think that the result of the repair of his left pyelo ureteral junction is perfect insofar as there is no dilatation of the calicheal cavities, the ureteral passages are excellent and there is simply a slightly chubby aspect of the pelvis, which is completely normal postoperatively.

The postoperative renal scan was also normal insofar as there was good emptying of the pelvis [...]. The curve is completely superimposable to that of the right kidney.

Regarding his vesico-renal reflux: on the right, the problem has been solved since the first operation by Dr. Favre in 1987. On the left, there was a narrowing of the terminal portion of the ureter, probably of ischemic origin, which justified a reimplantation in Bordeaux.

All that can be said at present is that there is no stricture at this level since the urography does not show ureteral dilatation. On the other hand, it is always theoretically possible to evoke a persistent reflux in the absence of a control cystography.

To try to close the debate and reassure the family, I asked for three retrograde cystograms in permictional and postmictional repletion, despite the numerous exposures that this child had already undergone.

In the absence of an image, I think we can conclude that her pain is anorganic, at least as far as the urinary tract is concerned, and possibly consider psychological care for this child, who is probably disturbed by everything that has happened to her, in the absence of any other sign of call on other tracts, particularly the digestive tract.

I need to see his mom again with the shots.

I will be sure to keep you informed.

Doctor Lemoine, urologist.

The narrowing of the ureter on the left, of ischemic origin, is perhaps due to the punches that this poor kidney was taking.

This doctor had good judgment on this story, it is obvious that my mother is not going to consider him competent enough and will want to keep us away from the truth about my pseudo illness.

And indeed, she brings me back to consult Dr. Verneuil, at the Bordeaux University Hospital, invoking a new pretext: hyperthermia. Perhaps she thinks that the pediatric surgeon is finally more manipulable than the urology surgeon?

March 7, 1990
To the attention of Dr. Pelletier, attending physician.

I am seeing Delphine Robin again today in consultation. She has presented this recent episode of hyperthermia, which probably

Fake background and punches

indicates an infectious episode. I think that the treatment you have started will solve her problem now.

The IVU and cystography you had performed show that there are good pyeloureteral passages without underlying dilatation and that there is no vesicoureteral reflux.

The scintigraphy that was done in Tours and that I recently received shows that there is an excellent slope of emptying of the two renal cavities and the two ureters, so I don't think that we can now incriminate stasis in the upper urinary tract in the genesis of this urinary infection. It is more likely to be a primary urinary tract infection in a child with a urological history. This type of phenomenon is seen quite often and I think the antibiotic treatment that you have instituted will be sufficient to resolve this problem.

For my part, I think that insofar as there was a new problem, it would perhaps be advisable to propose a cure or a small stay in a spa town for the next vacations so that she can rest because I found her a little tired this morning at the consultation.

Professor Verneuil, surgeon, Bordeaux University Hospital.

The exams show a very good kidney function, the doctors say I am fine, but my mother keeps trying to prove that I am sick and convinces me and everyone around me that I am not healthy.

I remember from this whole epic story that my mother was constantly worried about my condition. She is alarmist, so people who come to the house address me as if I were a fragile, weakened child, sometimes even as if it were the last time they would see me. I hate their kindness, their compassion, this image they have of me.

Mom also gets involved. When we come back from a consultation or hospitalization, I find gifts on my bed. They are given to me for no reason, just to please me, but it makes me feel like I don't have long to live.

But how does she manage to convince everyone that my health is dramatic when I am doing very well, as I can prove today, more than twenty years later?

The doctors continue to search, to examine me, referring to each other the little patient with the imaginary disease. I have imprecise memories of this period of wandering, I cannot connect certain images to the precise elements of my medical files, I do not remember the specialists I met, the establishments I went to.

I see a big office with carpet, I find myself once again naked in front of a doctor for an examination that I find very embarrassing, I am on the examination table, I see through the window a big city all lit up. Was it Niort, or Poitiers?

March 15, 1990
To the attention of Dr. Brunet, nephrologist, La Rochelle Hospital.

Thank you for referring little Delphine Robin to me for consultation. She is only 7 years old and her radiological file is already quite thick.

I've only seen a small part of it but I'll summarize his record this way:

- In October 1987, bilateral anti-reflux surgery of the Cohen type for, according to the mother, a bilateral stage III vesico-ureteral reflux after failure of a six-month medical treatment.

- Intravenous urogram of February 1989 which seems to me completely normal.

- Isotope scan of May 1989 which also seems to me to be completely normal.

- Re-intervention in June 1989 for an apparent stenosis of the left lower ureter.

- Intravenous urography of August 1989 which simply shows a large pelvis but without any dilatation of the calyces stems with completely concave calyces bottoms, thus without any sign of hyper-pressure in these cavities.

- September 1989, left pyeloplasty operation.

- CT scan of October 1989 which is normal.

- Isotope scintigraphy of January 1990 which shows a left curve shifted with respect to the right but with a completely parallel decrease, the non-overlap of the two curves being related to the greater volume of the cavities on the left.

- Intravenous urography of February 1990 which shows hypotonia of the cavities on the left side without however dilatation and with a ureteral passage; the cystography at that time does not show reflux.

This child complains about her left side but in fact, on examination, painful complaints are elicited by palpating both the pararachid musculature and the costal margin and therefore the renal origin of the pain may be questioned.

Finally, the parents are very worried and very much in need of a re-intervention which, in my opinion, is not necessary; for my part, I am not sure that I would have indicated the operation for the last two interventions.

I remain at your disposal to discuss this matter further.

Doctor Houzet, urologist, Niort clinic.

This doctor is asking questions that my mother doesn't want to hear, obsessed as she is with finding the genius specialist who would operate on me again. In fact, we will never go back to him and will continue our search for the "competent doctor".

March 16, 1990

To the attention of Professor Alain, urologist, CHU of Poitiers.

I was referred by the nephrologist, Dr. Brunet from La Rochelle. Delphine was operated in October 1987 for a bilateral reflux (according to Cohen's method) because she had urinary infections and fever repeatedly. She first had treatments for seven months without result, then the cysto showed a level four reflux, she had more infection. Very good on that side. She had a junctional problem that was operated on in September 1988. (The surgeon, Dr. Favre, is no longer in La Rochelle, for health reasons, he left).

Since January 1989, she started to have pain in her back again, always on the same side, which she made see on the left, she had treatments without result and the more time passed, the more she had pain.

When she pees, she has pain in her back upstairs.

She can hold it in, but it hurts her, it triggers big seizures, she needs to be given Spasfon.

I am also called from school.

There were fifteen days on Sunday, she had 39° all night, no sore throat, no ear, no stomach, just her back. On Monday the attending physician came, he could not touch her back, so she had six injections of Gentaline + Celestene, he sent me back to see the nephrologist Dr Brunet who found her tired, with dark circles around her eyes. He made her have a scintigraphy in January 1990, I carried the photocopy that I was given.

So we were supposed to come and see you on March 28, 1990, but he brought the appointment forward. Because on his last IVUS he found the left pelvis dilated, on the scan slower on the left.

So he told me that he knows you very well and that you certainly need to reconnect and he prefers that you do it.

Dr. Brunet explained to me that it is better to operate now than to wait until her kidney is affected, and we can't leave her like that.

Ms. Robin.

I am appalled. My mother herself wrote a letter to this urologist, to whom the nephrologist at the La Rochelle Hospital referred us, outlining his vision of my case and the consequences that it would entail. This taking of authority over the doctors, this will to impose

Fake background and punches

oneself in order to achieve one's ends leaves me devastated. Moreover, once again, she lies. She lies about the dates, places and reasons for the operations. But he will not play her game either.

March 16, 1990
To the attention of Dr. Brunet, nephrologist, La Rochelle Hospital.

I have just seen the child Robin Delphine, 7 years old, operated on in October 1987 for a bilateral vesico-renal reflux according to Cohen's technique, and then in September 1988, that is to say almost a year later, for an anomaly of the left pyelo-ureteral junction.

On a general level, this little girl is fine but she complains from time to time of her left lumbar fossa and had a feverish episode two weeks ago at 39°. Today's examination is completely normal. On retrograde cystography, there is no reflux and on intravenous urography the upper tract appears to me to be normal both on the right and on the left with, in particular, very good ureteral passages on the left, i.e. on the operated side. The impression is the same on the urography of August 19, 1989.

Finally, the urine is currently free of pus and germs.

I don't think we need to intervene on this little girl at all, and I suggest that you give her Nibiol syrup eight days a month.

I would like to see Delphine again for a consultation in three months.

Professor Alain, urologist, Poitiers University Hospital.

He did not see me again in consultation three months later. He did not find out what was wrong, he did not propose any operation: for my mother, he was ineffective.

The operation is the only good answer, her only concern, what she absolutely wants to obtain, against all medical diagnoses.

"We trust a mom"

Throughout my childhood, my mother tells me that my grandmother sees us from up there. Sometimes I wonder if she's watching us when Mom hits my side, when she tells me to show the doctor that my back hurts, when she falsifies urine tests, when she gets angry with the whip in her hand, or when she and her oldest son take great pleasure in humiliating and belittling my brother and me.

Why isn't she gentle and responsible like her own mother was? Mom often has big money problems. She is constantly borrowing from friends she knows well and from people in our family, always without my father knowing. She also regularly asks for food vouchers from the social service of the city hall. I am ashamed for her, I think that we must be pitied in the eyes of others. My mother seems to have it easy. She hides the financial difficulties from Dad, she takes care every day to go and collect the mail before he comes home from work so that he doesn't discover the possible letters of reminder for unpaid bills or for all the revolving credits she takes out.

She always takes her anger out on one of us, she takes turns on my father, one of my two brothers or me. It hurts me when my father is subjected to her contempt, her meanness. I don't understand why she behaves this way. She blames him for spending too much time on his volunteer work as a firefighter.

Anything that she doesn't control is blown out of proportion.

My alleged illness becomes for mom a source of concern more and more crazy. In the midst of conflicts and financial worries, she managed to drag me to Paris to see Professor Rodier again, armed with a letter from our attending physician and our nephrologist in La Rochelle, Dr. Brunet, who could not explain my pain in my left flank, since all my tests were normal.

The consultation will turn into a hospitalization that I have no memory of.

April 10, 1990
To the attention of Dr. Pelletier, attending physician.

We hospitalized Delphine Robin from April 10 to 12, 1990. During this hospitalization, a preoperative check-up was performed, including a blood count which showed a normal balance. The ECBU showed no abnormality.

Cystography performed on April 10 showed a normal distribution of digestive clears, opacification of a normal bladder. There was no vesico-ureteral reflux and no abnormality of the ureter or the bladder neck. We performed an endoscopy which showed a ureteral meatus stenosis and we performed a short meatostomy hoping that this procedure would improve Delphine's situation.

Professor Rodier, Necker-Enfants malades hospital.

We will not go to this doctor after this procedure.

April 25, 1990
To the attention of Dr. Hacquin, attending physician.

I am pleased to see Delphine Robin again today, who is not so bad after all, but who has had urinary problems again with pain in the lumbar fossa.

The examinations carried out today show that there is absolutely no dilatation of the upper apparatus, the emptying of his kidneys is strictly normal with precise opacification of the ureters and, with the Lasilix test, a complete emptying without stasis.

Since a cystography was done in March and was normal, I think that there is no longer a mechanical urological problem in this child. On the other hand, she still shows signs of bladder instability and I believe and persist in saying that she should be put on Ditropan to try to solve this problem because the instability alone can explain both the pain and the urinary infections that Delphine is starting to show again. On the other hand, I think that it would be desirable for her to go for a month's cure in a spa town during the summer vacations to try to improve her urinary system.

I will see Delphine again when you deem it useful.

Professor Verneuil, surgeon, Bordeaux University Hospital.

This is also the last consultation we will have with Professor Verneuil. I don't think Mom appreciates that he can't find any urinary problems that might require further surgery.

Moreover, during my research on my medical history, I discovered that a psychologist from Professor Verneuil's department had met me at the request of the specialist. I am surprised, I have no recollection of this and my mother has never spoken to me about it, but it must have reinforced her decision to stop seeing this doctor.

The psychologist recommended a family separation. Is this why Dr. Verneuil thinks it would be a good idea for me to undergo a treatment for a month? Is it a way to separate me and my mother?

This episode did not discourage her in any case and, one month later, we found ourselves in the office of a new urologist, at the Nantes University Hospital, Dr Brissaud. His secretary introduced us when he had not yet arrived. Mom took advantage of the fact that we were alone to give me her usual recommendations: tell him where I was suffering, make him understand that my kidney hurt when he examined me. I am afraid that he wants to make me undergo again all these examinations that I already underwent so much. I'm really fed up! My mother doesn't like to hear me say that I'm fed up, she always pretends that it's for my own good. And in my little girl's head, I tell myself that she wouldn't be wasting her time going around hospitals looking for a good doctor if it weren't so.

May 1990
To the attention of Dr. Pelletier, attending physician.

I saw your patient, Delphine Robin, 7 years old, for persistent left-sided back pain and a positive ECBU with Proteus.

The pain is triggered by the absorption of water and Lasilix.

This child underwent bilateral reflux surgery using Cohen's technique and pyeloureteral anastomosis in 1988. In spite of these interventions, left-sided lumbar pain persists.

On urography, there is a small retention of contrast medium in the left pelvis, but with some ureteral passages.

Cystography shows the absence of reflux.

The CT scan does not show a lesion of true chronic pyelonephritis in his left kidney, and this bodes well.

Clinically, there is pain in the left lumbar fossa, the rest of the clinical examination being strictly normal.

So we did an ultrasound of this left kidney, where we note a good renal parenchyma and relatively fine cavities. On the other hand, as soon as he was given enough water to absorb, the pyelo-caliceal cavities were clearly dilated. This is therefore in favor of the persistence of an obstacle at the level of its pyeloureteral junction.

I propose, in agreement with Mrs. Robin, to perform an inpatient DTPA scan which will show us a real functional value of her left kidney, [ ] the glomerular infiltration, [as well as] the quality of the urine flush from the pelvis to the ureter. The test is performed after intravenous injection with Lasilix. We therefore plan a date for this examination, and depending on it, we will make the decision of a new surgical correction or not.

Doctor Brissaud, urologist, Nantes University Hospital.

My mother lies! As she systematically does now. She claims that I was operated twice in La Rochelle, whereas the second operation took place in Bordeaux; she does not mention my passage to the clinic of Niort, nor the operations at the CHU of Poitiers or at the Necker hospital. However, it had only been a month since we had taken the medical excursion to Paris! She did not tell him about the consultation of February 6 with Dr. Lemoine, in La Rochelle.

Everything is wonderfully organized and allows mom to manipulate the doctors.

May 1990
To the attention of Dr. Brunet, nephrologist, La Rochelle Hospital.

Your patient, Delphine Robin, was admitted to the urology department on May 10 for a DTPA scan. Depending on the result of this scan, we had to plan an intervention or not.

The scintigraphy showed that there was an obstruction at the pyeloureteral junction. We therefore decided to intervene the next day. This operation was performed using the initial approach, with a slightly difficult dissection of the kidney due to postoperative fibrosis. After locating the downstream ureter, we went back to the renal pelvis where we were able to obtain a relatively correct dissection. We resected the initial anastomosis and redid the pyeloureteral anastomosis in a snowshoe fashion according to the Anderson technique. The junction was intubated with a Gil-Vernet drain that we maintained for ten days.

Delphine was discharged on the 18th, but was re-hospitalized for one day on May 25th to have the drain removed.

We agreed to see her again in consultation on July 25, with an intravenous urogram.

Professor Brissaud, urologist, Nantes University Hospital.

Yet the report of the radiologist who performed the DTPA kidney scan concludes with:

The DTPA scan did not reveal any evidence of a major obstructive syndrome.

This was my first hospitalization in this hospital. There will be many more.

In the meantime, a little respite is in order.

The school year is coming to an end and summer is a time when my mother leaves me alone. Every year she sends us to camp during the summer vacations, so that we can "leave her alone".

"I'm not going to put up with you for two months," she says each time.

Did I go to a cure that year as Professor Verneuil had recommended? I don't remember. Once again, my memories are confused.

But no matter where I went during these two months, what is sure is that as soon as I came back, the medical mops started again, and I found the sinister atmosphere of the house between an elder brother who always imposes his authoritarianism on his younger children, a father always so absent, and a mother who doesn't know how to manage neither the house, nor the money, nor her moods, and who, on top of that, imposes her obsessive madness on me.

August 1990

To the attention of Dr. Pelletier, attending physician.

I saw Delphine Robin, 7 years old, again in consultation. She had undergone a new left pyeloureteral junction plasty last May.

If everything was fine until then, she presented in the last few days an episode of cystitis with hematuria. An ultrasound was performed, showing that there was a small dilatation and ballooning of her pyelo-caliceal cavities, which is strictly normal.

There is a good passage at the lumbar ureter. We saw this today with an intravenous urogram, which showed a strictly normal pyeloureteral junction, a good injection of the ureter in the same way as on the right side.

This can be considered a good result of her junctional plasty for now. Her episode of cystitis quickly improved and should be ignored. In practice, we should leave Delphine alone as long as she continues to grow, and I will simply see her again in six months for a consultation.

Professor Brissaud, urologist, Nantes University Hospital.

"We must leave Delphine alone!

If only my mother had listened to the doctors, if only they had decided to stop all the investigations, maybe I would have been a little happy. I grew up too quickly, with the anguish of hospitals, of illness, of death, subjected to everything I was subjected to despite my revolt and my inner questioning.

But my mother is not interested in leaving me alone. I have to find out what my problem is and do something about it! What I don't understand is that no one checks what she says about the hematuria: only she sees it, the blood in my urine. But we believe her, of course, we can trust her, a mother only wants what is best for her child!

"We trust a mom"

I would like to continue going to school regularly, but even my schooling is not normal. I should have entered the second grade, found my teacher, my friends, but I repeated the year without knowing why and ended up with Paul in a school in a neighboring town where my mother found a job at the local hospital. This was convenient for her. She doesn't care about my academic success anyway, which is not her priority. I feel sad and angry, it is a suffering that is added to the others.

I would like to live my childhood like the others, I would like not to see any surgeon anymore, I would like her to stop asking me all these questions, to stop hitting me on the kidney.

While Dr. Brissaud did not want to see me again until six months later for a consultation, Mom brought me back to her office two months later.

October 1990
To the attention of Dr. Pelletier, attending physician.

I saw Delphine again in consultation with Robin, who had been operated on in La Rochelle several years ago for a left pyeloureteral junction plasty and an antireflux according to Cohen.

Postoperatively, he developed recurrent pyelonephritis and, in fact, a recurrence of his left pyeloureteral junction.

We therefore decided to perform a new plastic surgery.

At present, she is again presenting with left-sided lumbar pain, without any evidence of a recurrence of reflux [...].

I ask for a CT scan in order not to miss an infectious lesion in his renal parenchyma.

Doctor Brissaud, urologist, Nantes University Hospital.

Why doesn't the attending physician, who knows about my stay at the hospital in Bordeaux and the operations that were performed there, i.e. the antireflux and the junction plasty, draw Mr. Brissaud's attention to this? He probably thinks that mom did it: "You trust a mom, of course", he probably thinks.

Once again, the result of the scan is quite satisfactory.

But Mom keeps her mind on it, worse, she considers that the only way out for an effective cure is dialysis.

"Do you have pain in your kidney? When? Are you peeing well?"

She harasses me every day, continues to hit my side. She causes a persistent pain which confirms her hypothesis and justifies that she drags me again to the CHU of Nantes. Apparently, this year again my schooling is not going to be the priority.

October 1990
To the attention of Dr. Pelletier, attending physician.

In the absence of Dr. Brissaud, I have just seen little Robin Delphine, 7 years old.

She continues to have left-sided lumbar pain with febrile flare-ups despite the resumption of the junction plasty.

The urogram performed at the beginning of the month was quite satisfactory with beautiful pyeloureteral passages. Today I wanted to verify the absence of reflux by a cystography but it was not possible to catheterize her urethra.

I plan to admit Delphine for one day to perform a cystoscopy and cystography under a short general anesthesia.

P.-S.: I contacted the radiologists in La Rochelle who did not find any infectious foci in the renal parenchyma that could explain the recurrence of pyelonephritis.

Doctor Martin, Nantes University Hospital.

As I trace my history, I realize how many cystograms and urograms have been done. I find it impressive. I don't remember them all. I go back to that little girl's life, but I can't relive all the events I learn about as I go through this pile of papers; yet I find the inner pain I felt at the time, I remember how much I wanted to cry, scream, run away. But I always stayed and did exactly what was asked of me without any reluctance. I can place this little girl in "flashes": in a radio room; alone and naked on the table; in the consultation office; in the hospital room; at home... When I look back at this sometimes vague daily life, I sometimes look up and think: "The poor little girl, she must have been brave to endure all that without saying anything!"

I don't know if I accepted it to please Mom or because I really thought I was sick?

November 1990
To the attention of Dr. Pelletier, attending physician.

We took Robin Delphine back to the urology department. Despite a second pyeloplasty, she still has problems with low back pain on the left side of her body, and apparently has pain during urination.

We performed an intravenous urogram which was quite satisfactory, with good secretion from his left kidney, good pyeloureteral passages. It was not possible to perform a retrograde cystography. We therefore hospitalized her for one day in order to perform an endoscopy and to redo this retrograde cystography.

Endoscopy showed a normal bladder neck, ureteral orifices in place after his antireflux procedure. On the other hand, the cystography we performed was strictly normal, without reflux.

We can think that the persistence of the lumbar pain is linked to the two interventions that were performed on her left pyeloureteral junction and that the pelvis no longer distends when there is a significant water supply. There is no solution for Delphine for the moment. Unfortunately, we have to wait for the situation to evolve in one way or another.

Doctor Brissaud, urologist, Nantes University Hospital.

The function of my entire urinary and renal system is working properly, but the pain persists, which poses difficulties for the various doctors who are brought to see me. Why are these pains? How can I make them stop? Dr. Brissaud does not know what to do to help the little patient.

December 1990
To the attention of Ms. Robin.

I thank you already for the excellent oysters that you offered us. I am sending you a note about Delphine's hospitalization.

We therefore performed an intravenous urography under hyper-diuresis (injection of Lasilix) which showed by videoscopic study that there was an absence of dilatation at the level of her upper apparatus and a strictly normal ureteral flush with ureteral peristalsis without any anomaly at the level of her lower ureter.

The injection of Lasilix triggered a pain in Delphine similar to the one she presents. There was therefore no need to carry out any further investigations and we therefore injected an anaesthetic product (Xylocaine, Marcaine) at the level of her renal pedicle in the hope of making Delphine's pain disappear. The result of this injection will allow us to know if we should propose a denervation of her kidney if there is nothing else to do.

Doctor Brissaud, urologist, Nantes University Hospital.

Of course there's nothing else to do in mom's eyes.

December 1990
To the attention of Dr. Pelletier, attending physician.

Your patient Delphine Robin was rehospitalized in the department on December 17 to perform a denervation of her left kidney.

I injected Marcaine into the renal pedicle, which made a good improvement in the pain [ ]. We decided to perform this procedure by taking his left hypochondrial approach. This allowed us to clear his entire left kidney and completely free his vascular pedicle, cutting all neurological afferents.

The aftermath was then relatively correct for Delphine.

Delphine left the department on December 21.

Doctor Brissaud, urologist, Nantes University Hospital.

"I SEE NO OTHER SOLUTION
THAN THE REMOVAL OF THE LEFT KIDNEY"

We had a car accident. A car hit our car from behind, where I was sitting, alone. My father was driving, my mother was next to him.

The shock was not violent, but my mother was panicked. We went to the first bar we passed on our way, she took me to the bathroom, undressed; panicked, she told me there was blood, but I don't see anything, I don't know if she is lying or if there is really blood in the urine. The little girl wonders but once again lets herself be manipulated.

February 1991
To Dr. Brissaud, urologist, Nantes University Hospital.

Following a car accident on December 28, 1990, with left lumbar trauma, Delphine immediately presented with lumbar pain and hematuria. An emergency ultrasound was performed the same day. It did not show any abnormality but, in view of the persistence of this hematuria, a CT scan and a scintigraphy were performed. They

"I see no other solution than the removal of the left kidney"

showed a lumpy and non-functional left kidney. Hematuria still persists intermittently. Left renal artery lesion?

Should a left nephrectomy be considered?

Doctor Pelletier, attending physician.

February 1991

To the attention of Dr. Pelletier, attending physician.

I saw the child Robin Delphine again in consultation, with a DTPA scan and a CT scan.

There is indeed a major atrophy of his left kidney responsible for the hematuria and pyuria.

I find it difficult to explain this decrease in volume, but it is possible that it could be related to the trauma of the traffic accident. Unfortunately, I see no other solution than to proceed with the removal of his left kidney, after an endoscopic verification of the source of the hematuria. We are therefore planning this with Mrs. Robin, to hospitalize Delphine for about a week.

Doctor Brissaud, urologist, Nantes University Hospital.

Mom gets her way, I'm going to have a kidney removed. The punches she regularly throws at me have "paid off".

February 1991

To the attention of Dr. Pelletier, attending physician.

I therefore rehospitalized Delphine Robin on February 24, 1991 in the urology department.

I will just briefly review Delphine's clinical history. [Unfortunately, one month after the operation to remove her left kidney, a macroscopic hematuria appeared in the hours following a car accident. Mrs. Robin contacted me and I advised her to wait a little while to see if the hematuria would stop spontaneously. This was not the case and, in view of its persistence, you therefore ordered a CT scan and a DTPA scan which showed left renal hypovascularization associated with a significant decrease in left renal parenchyma.

In view of this finding, and after interviewing Mrs. Robin, I decided to carry out a new exploration of her left lumbar fossa. This operation was performed on February 25, 1991 [...]. We discovered a small, withered left kidney [...]. I therefore performed a left nephrectomy under duress. The postoperative aftermath was very simple for Delphine who left the department on March 3, 1991. Unfortunately, I still do not have the exact anatomical-pathological report, but I will send you our conclusions.

Doctor Brissaud, urologist, Nantes University Hospital.

Results of examinations prior to nephrectomy

Dtpa scan:
The conclusion:
- Well-vascularized but non-functioning left kidney (extremely low glomerular filtration).
- Right kidney slightly enlarged, well vascularized, with good glomerular filtration. There is stasis at the pyeloureteral junction, with intermittent emptying related to dilatation of the excretory urinary tract, but without real obstruction as shown by the Lasilix test.
At this point, given the significant functional deterioration of the left kidney and the functional quality of the right kidney, it may be worthwhile to perform a DMSA renal scan for a separate study of the functional value of each kidney (compensatory value of the left kidney).

Renal scan:

The conclusion:

- Bilateral renal secretion, but small humped left kidney.

- On the right, dilatation of the pelvis and cavities, without ureteral dilatation.

Pathology report (left kidney):

The conclusion:

- Acute and chronic ischemic lesions, with vascular damage of lesser intensity than these ischemic lesions would like. Stigmata of chronic ascending nephritis.

The return from surgery is terrible. I'm in pain, vomiting when I wake up. My bed rails are up. I would like my mom, sitting on a chair next to me, to lower them and hold me. But she didn't even make a gesture of comfort and went home as soon as the surgeon explained the operation to her.

I call the nurses, the orderlies, and I get from them what my mother doesn't give me. I always have the feeling that I am disturbing or annoying, but they don't reproach me, they come smiling. In the evening, I am anxious, I ask if I am going to die.

"Of course not."

But I am convinced that you don't tell a child that they are going to die. The nurses take the time to sit with me and soothe me, to hold my hand and tell me stories. The little girl thinks they want to give me a good time before she dies. This fear of disappearing has been ingrained in me since the day of this operation.

I understand that I have just had a kidney removed. From now on, Professor Brissaud wants to monitor the evolution of my single kidney. He explains to me that it would be desirable for it to develop in a more important way in order to compensate for the absence of the other one. It should become a large compensatory kidney. I am afraid and my mother does not reassure me:

"You can only live on dialysis when both of your kidneys are failing," she tells me.

She continues to worry about my health without giving me the comfort I need, this anxiety-provoking atmosphere permeates my whole being. She watches almost every TV show about organ donation with me. My father and brothers don't seem to be concerned about my upcoming death.

Since I am 8 years old, I am more and more anxious, I am very afraid that my right kidney will stop working suddenly. I often feel this way at night, when I go to bed. I fear that it will give out on me at night and that no one, not even me, will notice. This thought at the time scares me a lot. Sometimes I imagine the scene, Mom finding me dead in my bed. Even though I think she loves me, I also think she might be "happy" that I am dead. I imagine family and friends coming to see her whimpering, pitying her for having lost her child so sick for so many years. I realize that my mother appreciates the compassion that people around her have shown her since my kidney was removed.

During a consultation with the nephrologist at the hospital in La Rochelle, Mr. Brunet, I asked him if it was really possible to miss the diagnosis of the cessation of the function of my remaining kidney. He patiently and kindly explained to me that this could not happen suddenly, that before that, I could see edema appearing in my legs, that I would urinate less and less...

Since then, I have a ritual every night: I make sure I don't have edema in my legs the way the doctor showed me, and I go over my day in my head to make sure I've urinated regularly. Only then am I ready to crawl under the sheets.

But no, the fear invades me in spite of everything and keeps my eyes wide open in the darkness. So I leave my bedside lamp on, I sit up in bed so I don't fall asleep, I struggle, I'm tetanized at the thought of not waking up. Sometimes I am so overwhelmed that I can't keep my anxiety to myself. I get up and wake up Dad, I explain to him that I am afraid of dying, but he doesn't understand that I can have such

"I see no other solution than the removal of the left kidney"

thoughts. He ends up getting angry and orders me to go back to bed and sleep. Mom doesn't even wake up. I obey, without being the least bit reassured, and if I go back to bed, I don't fall asleep.

However, I always wake up the next day, happy not to have died, but unhappy not to have succeeded in resisting; I tell myself that it is at this moment that I could have died, at the moment when sleep defeated me in spite of myself. I arrive at school tired, I would prefer to stay at home, all alone, especially since the children make fun of me, of my school results, which are bad because of my repeated absences, and also of my clothes, which my mother has given to her at the time by the in-laws of one of her brothers, because she does not have the means to buy us new ones. They are out of fashion, a little worn, not in my size. I feel ashamed, I don't feel comfortable. I already have very little self-confidence in this school where I repeated a year and where I am unable to make friends with anyone. I feel sad and alone. I envy my classmates whose parents greet them at the end of school with a hug and a kiss, who are well dressed and work normally.

March 1991
To the attention of Dr. Pelletier, attending physician.

I received the complete anatomical-pathological examination of the nephrectomy specimen performed on Delphine Robin.
This histological examination shows large ischemic areas with zones of infarction leaving only ghostly tubular and glomerular structures. In other areas the parenchyma is better preserved and the glomeruli often have a completely retracted flocculus. On the other hand, its vessels are relatively unchanged, given the ischemic lesions observed. The arterioles are normal as well as most of the medium caliber arteries. At the level of the renal hilum, the veins are permeable, but some arteries show fibrous andarteritis that significantly narrows the luminal caliber.

In total, therefore, there are acute and chronic ischemic lesions with vascular lesions that are less intense than these ischemic lesions would like.

Consequently, I think that the association of a road accident and hematuria a few hours after this accident can be held responsible for the majority of the infarction or ischemic lesions found in the kidney.

Doctor Brissaud, urologist, Nantes University Hospital.

I can't help but think that the regular beating of my kidney for months may have caused the damage to my kidney.

Perhaps if, at the time, I had told Professor Brissaud about the way my mother was examining me by hitting me on the side, his conclusions about the anatomical-pathological analysis would have been different. But to talk to Professor Brissaud or even to someone else about my mother's behavior, her recommendations before the consultations, or the way the ECBU was done, would have been to betray her, to call into question her word as a "good mother". I gave her my kidney for love.

April 25, 1991
To the attention of Dr. Pelletier, attending physician.

I have just seen Delphine Robin again in consultation. I had performed a nephrectomy on her at the end of February 1991.

Healing is good, with a soft, if somewhat wide, scar, but this is not the case at the moment.

The most important thing is that Delphine no longer has any pain or abnormal urinary symptoms.

I have also seen the ultrasounds that you had done, which show a hypotonic pelvis, but this is strictly normal because it is extrasinusal and you have to wait until this kidney is in true compensatory hypertrophy.

"I see no other solution than the removal of the left kidney"

Finally, there is mostly a small but still moderate anemia.

Renal function is normal. The sedimentation rate is a little elevated, but this is not too worrisome because of the proximity of the procedure.

I will not give him a new appointment, but I will of course remain at your disposal should new elements arise.

Doctor Brissaud, Nantes University Hospital.

THE OBSESSION WITH A TRANSPLANT

Every time we leave the CHU in Nantes, we pass a large building that is part of the establishment. Mom says to me:

"Look, Nénette, you're going to go here one day."

This is apparently where dialysis patients and transplant patients go.

After school, some nights I go to my mother's workplace. She sits me down on a table, looks me straight in the eye and asks me if my back hurts, my kidney. It's a scene I remember vaguely, but one that several of my mother's colleagues who were there told me about.

"Yes, I'm in pain," I would routinely reply to my mother.

"Then you have to tell the doctor! How do you expect him to do the right thing if you don't say anything!"

How could she talk to me like that in front of people we hardly knew? Her colleagues tell me today that they didn't think it was normal, but that they didn't dare to intervene.

My mother's madness was beyond anyone's comprehension. Now that my left kidney had been removed, she was convinced that my right kidney was malfunctioning and began the search for that new sesame: the specialist who would accept the transplant or dialysis.

Under the pretext of fevers and pains, she brings me in emergency to the hospital of La Rochelle, in nephrology. Dr. Brunet, who usually takes care of us, is not there. Another nephrologist in the department examined me.

August 1991
To the attention of Dr. Pelletier, attending physician.

I received your patient, the child Robin Delphine, in hospital. [...] Since the left nephrectomy, Delphine continues to complain of right lumbar fossa pain in the context of a junctional anomaly on the right single kidney. This situation justified various complementary examinations which were not communicated to me by the family and which I did not find in the service file. However, I noted an episode of fever reaching 39° with back pain and dark urine in June 1991.

Recently, on Thursday, August 1, 1991, Delphine presented again with a fever of 39°, without significant lower urinary symptoms, which justified a treatment with Clamoxyl, after an injection of Lasilix, taking into account an oliguria.

In the ward on this Saturday, August 3, 1991, I noted pain on palpation of the right lumbar fossa, normal diuresis and apyrexia. Extemporaneous examination of the urine showed the absence of urinary tract infection, which should be confirmed by the laboratory. Humoral examinations (urea, ionogram, creatinine and nfs) were normal. The emergency ultrasound scan showed a right kidney of normal size, non-dilated cavities, a normal cortical index, a slightly blurred structure at the cortico-medullary junction (this aspect could correspond to an infectious pathology, but ultrasound is not a reliable examination in this field), the absence of a visible ureter and a semi-replete bladder, without any anomaly.

Given this information, I did not consider it necessary to prolong the hospitalization of this child with a long pathological history.

I simply proposed the continuation of a treatment. Of course, I maintained the appointment previously scheduled with Dr. Brunet, in the department.

Doctor Chauvin, nephrologist, La Rochelle Hospital.

Once again, the various tests done at the hospital were normal. This might make sense to my mother, but she is convinced that she has the key to the problem; the doctors who show her otherwise are incompetent in her eyes.

As usual, I don't say anything, I don't want to doubt her word; she loves me, she proves it by the way she struggles to find a doctor who will believe her.

She brought me back to the Nantes University Hospital for a consultation, as the emergency hospitalization in La Rochelle had not been successful.

August 1991
To the attention of Dr. Hacquin, attending physician.

I saw Delphine Robin in consultation, who had the problem of oliguria. In fact, this little girl has the problem of a lower urinary infection for which Clamoxyl was ineffective. The last scintigraphy was strictly normal, her right kidney must be completely cleared.

As a result, she has now been put on Bactrime which is better suited to the Proteus, yet her flow and urine are perfect today.

Delphine was reassured, and I simply asked her mother to come and see me again in six months.

Doctor Brissaud, urologist, Nantes University Hospital.

Mom doesn't know what to do anymore, she struggles body and soul to be heard.

August 1991
To Dr. Brissaud, urologist, Nantes University Hospital.

Delphine Robin has a urinary tract infection and is on Bactrime (oliguria, right lumbar pain).
So you will see her again for the evacuation disturbance; currently, this kid as well as the whole family are "lost".

Doctor Hacquin, attending physician.

In the midst of all this turmoil, I find some comfort in the beginning of the school year. I'm in CE1 this time and I'm going back to my old school, with my first teacher. Mom has indeed left her previous job, she is now working for the services of our municipality and is in charge of the maintenance of our school premises.

I am happy to be back with Mr. Pic. He is always so nice and treats me like any other child. He doesn't make fun of me or give me special treatment because I'm sick. It makes me feel good, I feel normal when I'm in his class and considered for myself. I make a lot of mistakes when I write, counting is still quite difficult and my addition and subtraction are quite bad. My mother finally noticed my shortcomings and discussed them with the teacher, who agreed to come to my house in the evening after school to try to help me catch up. His presence and support gave me back some confidence.

On the other hand, I can't find my old friends. They continued to move forward together in a class higher than mine. I still try to go back to them, but I feel that I am disturbing them. As for the children in my class, they seem too young to me, I don't want to be interested in them. During the first months, I stay sad and alone in the playground, or near my teacher if he is the one who watches us during recess.

October 1991

To the attention of Dr. Brissaud, Nantes University Hospital.

Delphine Robin continues to present almost permanent painful attacks on her right junction syndrome.

The ultrasound performed this day with a liquid injection test shows, compared to previous examinations, a dilatation of the calicium cavities.

If this dilatation gets worse, shouldn't we consider a plastic surgery? I therefore readdress it to you for consultation.

Doctor Brunet, nephrologist, La Rochelle Hospital.

I find myself hospitalized again, for the first operation on my right kidney. My mother doesn't realize how much I'm suffering. All these examinations, all these hospitalizations isolate me from the real world, from the other children. But she doesn't care, her only concern is to get a kidney transplant.

October 1991

To the attention of Dr. Pelletier, attending physician.

I therefore admitted Delphine Robin to the urology department on October 20 for treatment of her stenosis of the right pyeloureteral junction. I hesitated for a long time before intervening on this anomaly which seemed to me to be minor. Nevertheless, the existence of low back pain and the social context pushed me to make this decision, which was in fact a collegial decision since I had presented this file to the department's staff.

The procedure was performed through a small right anterior lumbar approach, allowing to clearly objectify the pyeloureteral junction. I then resected this junction, as well as a centimeter of ureter downstream, and made a perfectly permeable pyeloureteral junction. I then put in a pyelostomy drain as drainage, which allowed this anastomosis to heal quietly. I maintained this pyelostomy for ten days, at which time I clamped it and removed it. When the nephrostomy tube was removed, Delphine had some pain that was quickly relieved by the prescription of painkillers. In fact, the next night was perfect, as was the entire day, as Delphine drank copious amounts of water.

I therefore discharged her from the ward on October 31, for her home. I will see her again in consultation on January 8, 1992.

Doctor Brissaud, urologist, Nantes University Hospital.

These ten days of hospitalization are interminable for me. Being alone in this hospital bed depresses me. I often think about my friends, they are in class, they play, they live their life as a child. I think I'm the only one my age who is anxious and afraid of dying. I feel different from the others because of living in this adult world.

Mom calls me regularly, I beg her each time to come and get me. I hope she will realize that I am exhausted, that I feel worn out, that I can't take it anymore. But she doesn't seem to understand my distress, and I don't know what to do or say.

When she finally brings me home, I don't want to go back to school right away. I'm afraid the others will make fun of me, because I walk a little bent over because of the scar, which is quite big. Well, for my little girl's eyes anyway! So I stay alone at home, both my parents working and my brothers being at school. I appreciate the calm, but I quickly get bored. So I decided to do the housework, I don't mind and, above all, this way, my mother will realize that I am not so sick since I am able to activate myself immediately after the operation! But I don't have the impression that she thinks the way I would like. Her eldest son, on the other hand, is quick to point out that my health problems are "a sham". What does he care about? I blame him, it's probably easier to hate him than my own mother, whose energy for me I always hope proves that she loves me.

"She is a perfectly healthy child."

My mother obtained a "100% long term illness" for my "kidney disease", despite the questions of the medical officer about the distances travelled to ensure my medical follow-up. As usual, she had to be unfailingly insistent.

What to allow him to spend serenely the holidays of end of the year 1991. We go for the occasion to an uncle, a brother of mom, in the Paris region. But my mother never gives a break to her obsessions.

In my memories, I stay in bed most of the time. My mother tells me that I have a fever, she calls Dr. Brissaud to present the situation, probably exaggerating the reality to make it worrying. The celebrations were short-lived, we left in no time at all for the CHU in Nantes.

The doctor examined me as he usually does, looked at my kidney on the ultrasound. He tells me that I have to go to the operating room right away, that I have an abscess in my kidney. The little girl is in a deep anger. Angry at the doctor because I hate being caught off guard, not being warned. It's terrible for me not to have time to get used to the idea of hospitalization. I am tired of all these operations, I am afraid of being asleep, of not waking up. This umpteenth operation makes me anxious, but I have to accept it, I have no choice.

As usual, it is a difficult ordeal, going to the operating room is nerve-wracking. "My room, always the same, the shower, the hospital gown, the little slippers, the cap, the premedication that I have to take lying on the bed, everything is a torture. I am very tense, I am so cold that I am shivering. The premedication is supposed to relax me, but I'm still so scared.

"I'm scared, I don't want to go," I tell my mom, who is next to me, until they come to get me and take me to the OR.

The bed rolls, I walk for a long time in a corridor, I see the lights above me passing slowly. The nurses pushing the bed are talking about banal things, about their life, their work... I am frozen, terrified by what awaits me.

We arrive in front of the door of the block, the team which accompanies me rings, introduces itself, the doors open.

The nurses must notice that I am worried, they try to reassure me, they speak to me gently, kindly, they caress my forehead, but this does not soothe me at all, I don't care about their kindness, I want to leave here! I don't like it when they tell me at the sight of my file, which is placed at the foot of my bed:

"You must be used to it, you know how it goes, don't be afraid, just relax."

I'm being carried to the operating table, I'm shaking with cold or fear. I want to see everything that is done to me, I look at everything, I have the impression that it is swarming with people around me, I don't know if there are really so many people or if it is my imagination playing tricks on me.

They put an IV in me, they ask me to turn my head so I can't see the needle, but I'm not afraid of needles, I want to watch. They put cold round patches on my chest, connect wires to them, put a clip on my finger, a cuff on my arm for blood pressure, and put a warm sheet over my naked body, completely frozen.

I ask to be warned when I am going to be anaesthetized. I want to know, to be ready, I hate this moment even if it is very short; I feel myself leaving, it is a very unpleasant sensation.

Before falling asleep, I see Mr. Brissaud putting on his surgeon's coat. He sends me a little note with a smile, it touches me, but I don't feel like smiling at all; even if I did, I don't think I could because I am so tense.

The return from the operating room was catastrophic; each time I lived the same hell: I vomited, my kidney hurt, my scar hurt. My throat hurt too, they had to insert a tube while I was sleeping.

When I arrive in my room, mom is there, waiting for me, sitting on a chair. The barriers of my bed are assembled, I do not cease turning to the left, to the right, by clinging to it, I have pain in the back without mom having needed to strike me.

"I'm scared, I'm in pain, go tell them I'm in pain, please!"

But Mom doesn't really react.

"It's normal, you've just been operated on, we've just touched your kidney. There must be something to calm the pain in your IV," she simply replied.

January 1992

To the attention of Dr. Pelletier, attending physician.

So I managed to re-hospitalize Delphine in the urology department, in order to find out what was really going on with this right renal problem. My first surprise, when I saw her, was to find her in good general condition, whereas the mother was sending me daily signals and the creatinine figure made us think of the institution of a renal insufficiency.

I saw the latest ultrasound and arteriogram, which prompted me to admit Delphine to the hospital in order to get this story completely straight.

To do this, we first performed a blood test under general anesthesia, which was immediately reassuring, since the creatinine level we noted was 48 mmol (the normal range is 30 to 75). On the other hand, we placed a right nephrostomy drain under

"She is a perfectly healthy child."

I understand that at the time Mr. Brissaud lied to us, that he used this kidney abscess as a pretext to be able to carry out benign examinations under general anaesthesia, allowing to show that my kidney was functioning well. Did he want this to be done in the hospital, without my mother being able to participate in anything, to protect me?

Did Mom know that I didn't have surgery for an abscessed kidney?

How did Mr. Brissaud make this operation look like it really happened? The scar? The bandage?

My mother always lifts the sheets when I come back from surgery, she examines my dressing, the catheter... She should have realized something, right?

She waits to see Mr. Brissaud who always comes by in the afternoon after the surgery. Then, she goes back home, pretending that she has to take care of the two others. I don't notice her absence too much, I sleep almost all the rest of the day.

The following days seem long, I am abandoned there, all alone. My companions are the television, my coloring book and the nurses. I ask that the door be left wide open at all times, I feel less alone, the room where the nurses meet is right across from my room.

The days are almost always the same, everything is set up like clockwork.

I wake up early in the morning, I hear the nurses talking in the hallway. They bring me breakfast, I eat in bed, all alone.

A little later in the morning, someone comes to wash me. I hate this moment. I lay in my bed, the nurses wash me with a glove that they wet in a basin, they wash me from head to toe. They turn me on my side to wash my back, then they pass me the cologne left by mom; it's cold, and I don't like the smell. It is really a humiliating moment, I would like to tell them to leave me alone, I would like to call mom to come and get me, but I let them do it without protesting, I remain silent. I feel unhappy. I would rather be at home, wash myself, go to school.

Then came the time for the dressing, which was also difficult. I am apprehensive about the care I am about to receive and I ask a lot of questions while the nurse takes care of me. Before she rips off the bandage to clean my scar, I ask her if it will hurt; when she lightly pulls on something that looks like a piece of rubber to make it move, I ask her if it will be removed today, along with my IV. She also takes care of emptying my pee bag: there is a hole right next to my scar with a hose and a bag where urine is collected. She then sticks a new bandage on. Finally, she changes my sheets; during this time, I either lie in my bed or sit in a chair next to the bed.

The nurses tell me that I am a very brave little girl. The compliment pleases me, but I don't answer anything, I just smile a little politely.

At the end of the morning, it is the visit of the doctor. Mr. Brissaud came to my room with several people, the nurse and students. He asks me a few questions to know if I am well, if I slept well, if I have any pain. I answer with nods and a little smile.

At lunchtime, the nurses come and ask me if I want to get up to go eat in the playroom, which is located between the two children's rooms on the ward. I always refuse, I want to stay in my bed, I want to be left alone.

The afternoon is long: nothing happens anymore, I stay lying down watching TV, coloring, sleeping, crying... I am sad, lost, distraught

In the middle of the afternoon, I am offered a snack but I am not hungry or thirsty. They insist that I take something to drink, so I take a fruit juice.

In the evening, mom calls on the nurses' extension, they pass the call to me in my room. If I find it takes a long time before she calls, I ask the nurses to call her. Sometimes they refuse, explaining to me that I have to be patient, but it has already happened that they agree to give me the handset so that I can anticipate mom's call.

Every time I get him on the phone, I cry. I imagine the four of them, my parents and my brothers, how good they must be together at home. I beg her to come and get me right away. She tells me it's not possible, that it's far away, but that soon she will come.

I find myself alone in front of my evening meal, I am not hungry but I force myself.

It's time to go to sleep, but I don't want to be in the dark, I don't want to hear a sound, to be alone. I always keep the bedroom door and the window shutter open. The city of Nantes all lit up is beautiful and brings me some comfort. I also leave the TV on so that it makes a presence.

During the night, I am woken up several times by the nurses coming to make sure that everything is going well, blood pressure, infusion...

I remember one night I was very agitated. I keep calling the nurses, I don't want to be alone, I want to go home right away, I want to call my mom and have her come and get me. I don't care how far away it is, I don't care how late it is to call her, if she's mad at me for waking her up, I really want her to pick me up tonight!

Finally a nurse stays with me for a while, sits next to my bed and holds my hand until I fall back to sleep. Mom never does this when I'm afraid to sleep; she doesn't even get up to check on me when I call her in the middle of the night.

The "rubber" is removed on the day of my discharge. This is good news, but also a very dreaded moment. I listen to the footsteps approaching my room, I am not in a hurry for the nurse to arrive. When they take out the tube, or the catheter, it feels like they are taking out everything in my stomach. I am tense, I am afraid of being in pain, I am hot.

The paramedic takes me home. I am alone with him. Mom didn't come to pick me up.

"Münchhausen syndrome by proxy"

February 13, 1992
To the attention of Dr. Pelletier, attending physician.

I see Delphine again in consultation, who, on the pure renal level, poses few problems.

Indeed, the renal function is currently normal.

I did a follow-up ultrasound which shows a normal kidney [...]. There are good ureteral passages and good ureteral contraction.

There is always the problem of pain, which is mainly posterior in the lumbar region, and we cannot exclude a neurological problem, in particular an intercostal nerve injury.

I have asked Mrs. Robin to give us some time to see how things will evolve. I will see Delphine again at least at the end of the school year, to see if we can't try an anesthetic block of the intercostal nerve, by cutaneous injection.

If this blockage by Xylocaine or by a Xylocaine/Marcaine mixture is positive, it would certainly be interesting to see Dr Biron, in order to perform an alcoholization of this neurological root. I think that

*this is a much more interesting solution than planning any surgery
that has little chance of success.*

Doctor Brissaud, urologist, Nantes University Hospital.

At that time, Mom still talks about dialysis, transplants, organ
donation...

"Your brothers could eventually donate one of their kidneys to
you," she said to me one day.

I'm furious, there's no way I'm going to get a kidney transplant,
let alone one from her oldest son! I think she is crazy to imagine
this teenager that I hate giving me one of his organs, rotten on
cigarettes and drugs. I don't want anything from him or anyone
else for that matter. I want to live forever with my one kidney.

She also gets it into her head that I have diabetes problems.
She regularly sees a doctor for herself, apparently there is a history
of it in her family, and she has diabetes treated with medication,
following the shock of her mother's death, she claims.

February 28, 1992
To the attention of Dr. Pelletier, attending physician.

I saw Delphine Robin, 9 years old, in consultation today.

*This young girl presents the problem of a recently discovered diabetic
state with a fasting blood glucose level of 1.49 g/l on February 7 and a
value of 1.52 g/l on February 19 measured under the same conditions.
Many antecedents of non-insulin-dependent diabetes in his family (his
mother, his aunt, his maternal grandfather). There was no weight loss.
The clinical examination did not provide any additional information.*

*The age of this patient would argue for insulin dependence. The
family history, the absence of clinical signs of insulinopenia, the
stability of blood glucose values at fortnightly intervals and the absence
of ketonuria, plead on the other hand for a non-insulin dependence.*

Delphine is currently very reluctant to be hospitalized again because of her renal history. However, we have agreed on a day hospitalization on a Wednesday in order to finalize the dietary measures to be advocated, to teach Delphine and her mother the technique of self-monitoring of blood sugar and to introduce probably in a first step a treatment with oral antidiabetic drugs, preferably using an adequate treatment in case of renal insufficiency.

Doctor Gallais, diabetologist, La Rochelle Hospital.

We don't need to be taught the technique of self-monitoring of blood sugar, my mother already has a device to check her blood sugar at home. Even before she went to see this doctor, it became her new obsession. She regularly pricks my fingertips to check my blood sugar. I have to admit that at first I'm amused, but after a while I get really fed up, especially since I can see that she's getting into the game. She believes in it like crazy, she talks about it all the time: I'm diabetic, it's hereditary! It seems to me that this pleases her, I find it strange that she is happy about my illnesses.

According to the study of my medical records, Mr. Brissaud was not informed of this consultation with the diabetologist. He continues to discover a "microbe" in my urine and to prescribe syrups and tablets.

May 4, 1992
To the attention of Ms. Robin.

While we were desperately waiting to have a urine cytobacteriological examination done on Delphine, I submitted the case to the nephrology department to see what they thought of Delphine's albuminuria problem.

This albuminuria starts to be significant and two etiologies can be retained:

The first is that of a diabetic origin, which is unlikely at the present time.

The second possibility is that this albuminuria is due to the vesico-ureteral reflux that Delphine had, and that the protein losses are only related to the abnormalities caused by this reflux, which is quite often visible.

In order to assess the situation, the nephrologist would like you to carry out a number of biological tests on Delphine. All of these tests are recorded on the prescription I am sending you. As far as the 24-hour urine collection is concerned, I am sending you a supplementary sheet that explains how to perform these tests. We are therefore waiting for these results in order to make a decision.

Doctor Brissaud, urologist, Nantes University Hospital.

Mr. Brissaud presented my file to a nephrologist at the nephrology department of the Nantes University Hospital because he began to doubt my mother's credibility. He began to set up a strategy to "trap" her.

June 8, 1992
To the attention of Dr. Hacquin, attending physician.

I saw in consultation the child Robin Delphine that you referred to me for a renal ultrasound, because of anuria since three days according to the parents.

This child underwent a left nephrectomy in February 1991 in Nantes for a problem of junction syndrome and vesico-ureteral reflux, after a first operation in La Rochelle in 1987.

When she entered, she had the urge to urinate, there were 280 ml of urine.

Clinical examination shows a discrete pain on palpation in the left and right flank.

Renal ultrasound was not required.

Doctor Antonescu, pediatrician, Rochefort hospital.

I don't remember this consultation, yet mom must have been furious, I didn't obey her usual instructions. This is one more sign that tightens the noose around her lies.

The doubt of Mr. Brissaud on the veracity of the symptoms invoked by mom leads him to present my file to two doctors of the mother and child hospital of the CHRU (regional university hospital center) of Nantes: Doctor Gauthier, nephropediatrician, and Doctor Carrez, child psychiatrist.

July 22, 1992
To the attention of Ms. Robin.

I would like to see Delphine again in consultation with Dr. Carrez, a child psychiatrist.

If this date does not suit you, you should write to me, you will not be able to call me because I am on vacation.

I hope Delphine is well.

Doctor Gauthier, specialist in pediatric nephrology,
mother and child hospital, CHRU of Nantes.

August 10, 1992
Dr. Gauthier,

I'm responding to your post, we won't be able to come on August 21 because I've just been working since June 1 so I can't ask for too much, so I cancelled the appointment.

"Münchhausen syndrome by proxy"

I had Mr. Brissaud on the phone, we explained: I will take a blood and urine test every three months and I will send him the original, and we will go to see him every month in consultation, we agreed like that, he sent me a prescription for blood and urine test, he will have the original and we have an appointment on September 9, 1992 in consultation with him. You will be informed by Mr. Brissaud. Delphine is fine, she's enjoying her vacations, we're going to the beach, we're going for a walk... except that she has some burning and urinary leakage, but nothing at all. As for the doctor treating her, you gave me your word not to talk about it, I never want to tell him, I count on your word, since we arranged with Mr. Brissaud, I will send him all the originals of the examinations.

So I count on you, thank you.

Ms. Robin.

Mom understands what this is all about. She refuses the idea of a consultation with a psychiatrist. She seems upset, worried.

September 11, 1992
To the attention of Dr. Hacquin, attending physician.

I see Delphine in consultation today. The situation, clinically speaking, is quite satisfactory. The ECBU still shows a few germs but this has no impact and I agree with you that we should not treat. Biologically, the situation is also quite reassuring.

The ultrasound showed a right kidney without significant pelvic dilatation. I explained to Mrs. Robin that, for the time being, we would leave it at that, and that I would not see Delphine again until next summer to see if the situation was evolving well.

I am also sending the results of the biological tests to Dr. Gauthier, a pediatric urologist, so that he can confirm my feeling.

Doctor Brissaud, urologist, Nantes University Hospital.

September 14, 1992

To Dr. Brissaud, urologist, Nantes University Hospital.

As I already had the opportunity to tell you orally, I saw last July Miss Robin Delphine that you had referred to me for a renal insufficiency with "anuria" noted by the mother.

The examination of his very busy history, as well as the study of the laboratory sheets brought by the mother, made it easy to make the diagnosis of Münchhausen by proxy syndrome. Indeed, on the sheet of the examinations undertaken on June 29, 1992, it was noticed that the creatinine had been modified and that a "2" had been added in front of the 6.7 mg/l, which, of course, changed the problem considerably; moreover, Mrs. Robin very quickly "confessed" these modifications of creatinine. The same applies to sodium at the examination of June 17, 1992, since the natraemia was 185 mmol/l, which of course was completely incompatible with the clinical data...

This rather extraordinary story needs to be taken care of by our psychiatric colleagues.

Indeed, the heaviness of the therapies initially undertaken and the disturbances that this child underwent cannot be resolved by a simple follow-up in urological consultation.

I received on August 10, 1992 a letter from Mrs. Robin telling me that Delphine was going to be followed again by Mr. Brissaud and that she was to see him again on September 9 with regular consultations at his place. I believe in fact that the major problem of Mrs. Robin is that she obliges herself to a psychiatric follow-up and I thus write to her again that I wish to see her again with my colleague of child psychiatry, Doctor Carrez, at the end of August. It is absolutely necessary that she comes to the consultation.

If Ms. Robin did not come to counseling, then I believe that a social action measure would be taken to limit any adverse effects of this very troubled mother on her child.

Doctor Gauthier, specialist in pediatric nephrology, mother and child hospital, CHRU of Nantes.

"This child and this family need to be supervised"

For weeks, my mother avoided the confrontation with Dr. Gauthier and Dr. Carrez, not answering the reminders, or cancelling at the last minute the appointments that had been scheduled. She felt that the wind was turning and that the noose was tightening around her.

October 19, 1992
To the attention of Ms. Robin.

I have received your message asking me to cancel the October 8, 1992 consultation with us.

Nevertheless, it seems essential to me that I can see Delphine and yourself with Dr. Michel Carrez before November 1st. In these conditions I ask you to make a consultation appointment as soon as possible.

In the absence of a favorable response from you, I will be obliged to take any action I deem useful to preserve Delphine's health.

Doctor Gauthier, specialist in pediatric nephrology, mother and child hospital, CHRU of Nantes.

Mom no longer has a choice. We meet with the two doctors at the end of December.

During the interview, they ask to speak to my mother alone. I sense that they don't like her very much, their cold anger is so noticeable that it becomes ingrained in my childhood memory, even though I have no memory of their physical appearance. I understand that something serious is happening. I refuse to leave my mother, I resist to stay in the office, but the doctors are stronger than me. I find myself outside the room, clinging desperately to the closed door handle, crying.

The little girl wonders if they are going to punish her mother because of what she did a few weeks ago with her older son. While I was out of school, they sat at the dining room table. Mom is holding the latest lab results and a double-sided eraser. I'm on the couch, pretending to watch TV, the corner of my eye screwed on them, my ear to the ground. The way they're acting, I have a feeling they're plotting something.

"Are you sure it won't show?" my mom asks her oldest child.

I don't ask them any questions, but I understood that they were falsifying my results.

December 23, 1992
To the attention of Dr. Gauthier, nephropediatrician, CHU de Nantes, for transmission to the children's judge.

This is a child who has been followed for quite a long time by Dr. Claude Gauthier and who has experienced a series of rather tragic events. That is, after chronic paralumbar pain, after an attempt at peri-renal analgesia, she lost a kidney and a nephrectomy had to be performed.

The whole thing is now undoubtedly part of a Münchhausen syndrome.

Today's consultation has been scheduled for a long time, but we had to call this mother several times before she followed through.

The consultation should allow us to make some progress and in particular to obtain that mother and daughter can be followed from now on.

Indeed, it is inconceivable to "leave them in the wild". This child and this family must be supervised and in particular by the services of the judge of the children so that one does not launch out again in a therapeutic escalation or rather iatrogenic.

The mother has finally come to terms with her own problems and, as is fairly typical, when we start to unravel the reality, she goes on to explain how she doctored the creatinine results she was presenting to Claude Gauthier.

A triple intervention will be planned at the level of the judge of the children, the general practitioner and the intersecteur of infantile psychiatry.

Indeed, we learn that Delphine is an extremely fearful child and always extremely close and "stuck" to her mother.

We also learn that the older boy in the family has problems such as successive school expulsions and behavioral problems. In such cases, I prefer to be a little "ahead" of the events before they happen and I discuss with this woman the problem of her reactions to today's interview by telling her that I would not want her to "do anything stupid" either. She understands what I mean by that and says that there is no question of her committing suicide. She plans to return to a psychiatrist near her home.

She herself will, according to our advice and in all probability, notify the children's judge while we will do it on our side.

Doctor Carrez, child psychiatrist.

This period marked a real change for me and for my whole family. It was no longer my case that the doctors were examining, but that of my mother, who was gradually losing her footing. Reality caught up with her and our home became an object of judicial concern.

"This child and this family need to be supervised"

January 13, 1993

To the attention of the Juvenile Court Judge, Rochefort District Court.

We hereby bring to your attention the case of the child Robin Delphine.

This child was caught in the process of what we medically call a "Münchhausen by proxy syndrome".

That is, her mother distorted several consecutive medical examinations and formulated successive complaints in her daughter's place. These complaints concerned the urinary tract. So much so that a series of examinations were proposed which led to an infiltration of a peri-renal zone, an infiltration which was itself complicated and which required the removal of a kidney.

We regularly encounter such cases.

We felt it was important that you were able to receive and help this family because we do not see how there could not be supervision or protection of the child.

We have advised Ms. Robin to contact you, which she may have done by the time we write.

The child is also inhibited, anxious; she needs child psychiatric help. I informed Dr. Florent, head of the child psychiatry department at the hospital in Saintes, about this.

Doctor Gauthier, specialist in pediatric nephrology and Doctor Carrez, child psychiatrist.

January 15, 1993

To the attention of Dr. Hacquin, attending physician.

I saw Delphine Robin again in consultation on December 28. I had not informed you of her medical problems until now at the request of Mrs. Robin who did not wish to divulge the last diagnosis made in her daughter and in her home. Indeed, when I was brought to see Delphine for the first time in September 1992 at the request of my colleagues in urology, I quickly realized that we were facing a Münchhausen syndrome by proxy. You will find a copy of the letter sent on September 14, 1992 to Professor Brissaud. Indeed, Mrs Robin had falsified the creatinine results, and I think that all the previous history concerning the renal problems presented by her daughter is related to reasons invoked by the mother and the daughter and not to real reasons of somatic disease.

After a meeting with the child psychiatrist, Doctor Carrez, it was agreed to inform the judge of the children. You will find enclosed the duplicate of the letter sent to him and recorded by myself and Dr. Carrez, child psychiatrist at the University Hospital of Nantes.

It is therefore important that you follow up regularly with Delphine, knowing the context. I believe that the family environment is very fragile and requires regular support from you. Psychiatric support for Delphine is also planned by a child psychiatrist in Saintes.

All in all: Münchhausen syndrome by proxy, absence of real somatic impairment encountered in Delphine, disorders "invented by the mother".

Doctor Gauthier, specialist in pediatric nephrology, mother and child hospital, CHRU of Nantes.

Dr. Gauthier also alerts the educator who is to meet with me and communicates to him all the exchanges that have taken place between our attending physician and Professor Brissaud.

The situation at home is becoming more and more complicated, I don't really understand what is going on, but I realize that Mom is worried, I hear talk of separation, of going to live elsewhere, of leaving my family. This prospect terrifies me, I want to stay at home.

Already more or less depressed, I see my mother taking pills more and more often. Sometimes she wakes up at night, completely

"This child and this family need to be supervised"

panicked. From my room, I hear everything. The doctor comes, gives her a shot, reassures her and leaves. I would be unhappy to let her down, to give her more reasons to be anxious if I had to leave. The doctors may want this separation; for my sake, they think it's helpful, but they don't really think about Mom, how sad she will be. They don't know how bad she is. I hear her talking about dying, "I'd be better off if I wasn't here anymore, I wouldn't piss anyone off."

I don't want her to do something stupid because of me.

June 9, 1993
To the attention of Dr. Carrez, child psychiatrist at the CHU of Nantes.

I received your letter concerning the young Delphine Robin for whom you spoke of a Münchhausen syndrome by proxy.

Faced with the perplexity of my team but also of the juvenile judge's department, I am led to ask you for much more precise elements concerning the clinical history and the succession of incidents that led to the removal of the left kidney.

I received Mrs. Robin and her daughter, the situation seems to me all the more worrying as a new renal intervention on the remaining kidney is envisaged and Mrs. Robin is considering a transplant in the future.

Therefore, in order for me to work with the family and the services that will meet with them, I would be very grateful if you could send me an extremely complete clinical summary or, preferably, communicate the file to me in confidence if possible.

Doctor Florent, child psychiatrist at the hospital of Saintes.

I don't remember this doctor, but I'm not surprised by his perplexity about this diagnosis. It is hard to believe that a doctor would remove a little girl's kidney because of a manipulative mother.

June 11, 1993
To the attention of Dr. Hacquin, attending physician.

I had recently sent you a letter concerning the child Delphine Robin, for whom you are the general practitioner.

This child has a serious organic and psychological problem.

You must have been made aware of the diagnosis made at the Nantes University Hospital of a mother-daughter relationship pathology.

I was able to contact Mrs. Robin and her daughter and I would like to verify the validity of this diagnosis.

Could you give me some information about some of the medical records and circumstances that led to the child's kidney removal? I do think that Delphine needs psychotherapeutic work to help her resolve her overwhelming anxiety.

Doctor Florent, child psychiatrist at the hospital of Saintes.

According to my memories I was brought to see a psychologist at the Centre d'aide médico-psychologique à l'enfance (CAMPE) in Marennes. Perhaps it was through this child psychiatrist, Dr. Florent?

I have a feeling that she thinks what mom does for me is not right; the little girl in me doesn't want anyone to think that, I want her to be seen by others as a loving and caring mom. I alone have the right to think that she sometimes exaggerates events, but I take all the precautions I can to protect her from people who judge her negatively. So, from the very first consultation I want to flee, to have nothing more to do with this psychologist. I start to get up from my chair, but immediately sit down again. The wise child takes over: it is up to her to tell me when I should leave.

"Do you want to leave, Delphine?" the CAMPE psychologist asks me.

"No, no, I'm sitting back down fine."

When I see her again, she asks me if my UTIs come at particular times. I pretended not to understand the question, so she clarified it: "Do they occur on specific days of the week? Now I really don't think that's a good idea. Why would there be special days? I understand that she wants to make me say things that will lead to my mother's separation. I still believe that Mom could never hurt me, despite what everyone we meet seems to think at the moment. She's the one who's right, it's the shrink who's really wrong! This time, I get up from my chair without warning her, quickly walk out of the office and throw to Mom who is waiting for me on the landing, "Quick, let's go!"

September 6, 1993
To Dr. Florent, child psychiatrist.

Mr. Doctor,
I have just received a letter giving me an appointment for my daughter Delphine on Friday 17 September 1993 at 9.30 am. We are starting a new school year and I don't want Delphine to miss classes because she is already late enough. I would like appointments outside of school hours (Wednesday or school vacations). Delphine did not want to go to the last interviews with the CAMPE psychologist, is there any point in continuing against her will? Please keep us informed.

Ms. Robin.

I probably continued to evolve by preferring to repress my emotional pain. Surely this is the only way to survive in an unbearable situation. All these memories, this powerlessness, this humiliation caused by all these examinations where each time I found myself naked in front of mom and doctors, I wanted to scream but I couldn't, I wanted to tell mom that I would prefer that this stops, that she gets mad at me for lying, for exaggerating but I couldn't do it either.

I idealized Mom, I was convinced that she loved me, otherwise why would she struggle like she did?

However, she often has impulsive reactions, such as the slap that leaves without any notice or explanation, for futile reasons. There is also her passivity in front of her son, when he insults me or when he also has excesses of violence towards me: he grabs me by the hair and speaks very close to my face, to make sure that I understand him well. He makes sure that authority reigns with him.

My father, on the other hand, I feel nothing for him, neither love nor hate. I don't understand him: why doesn't he stop them from acting like that? Maybe he doesn't like me? He would prefer to have a girl who is not sick? he does not find me interesting? I ask myself all these questions in my childish head, but I do not dare to ask him, I prefer not to know the truth. And then, he speaks to me very little, and, consequently, I also speak to him very little; I know that it is very strange, but I do not like when our eyes meet.

October 8, 1993
To Dr. Brunet, copies to the Children's Judge and Dr. Hacquin.

Here is some additional information about the young Robin Delphine that you had the opportunity to see for "high blood pressure".

I knew this little girl for the first time on July 1, 1992, the day my colleagues in urology and adult nephrology referred her to me for renal insufficiency with anuria. The results of the examination - undertaken on June 17, 1992 by a medical analysis laboratory -, brought by the mother, had obviously been tampered with and a

"This child and this family need to be supervised"

"1" had been added in front of the creatinine level, which of course changed things completely, the true creatinine being 6.5 mg/l. When I took her history, I quickly realized that it was a Münchhausen syndrome by proxy. Moreover, Mrs. Robin quickly admitted to me that she had manipulated a large number of complementary examinations. In these conditions, a meeting with Doctor Carrez, child psychiatrist of the service, allowed to put things in order, and we warned, by a common letter on June 13, 1993, Mrs Garnier, judge of the children at the court of first instance of Rochefort. Theoretically, Delphine and her family were also to be followed by Mr. Lefebvre, an educator at the courthouse in Rochefort.

If new somatic manifestations were to be found in Delphine, it would be very important to establish a workup in a pediatric hospital in order to determine the cause of this possible high blood pressure. From what you have told me, there have already been several kidney scans, which could have medico-legal implications for the doctors who ordered them.

In agreement with Doctor Carrez, it seems to me highly important that Delphine be hospitalized again in a pediatric service, either in Nantes, which I would like, or in Tours at my friend Hugues Neveu's, whom I will immediately inform if you decide to transfer her to Tours. In any case, this little girl is in danger and it is absolutely necessary to stop this infernal circle of consultations and hospitalizations based on maternal descriptions.

I am sending a copy of this letter to the children's judge and I hope that you will be able to tell me quickly what you plan to do with this child.

Furthermore, I am sending you all the photocopies of the letters that I have sent to the various people involved since my first consultation with this little girl.

Doctor Gauthier.

To the attention of the Juvenile Judge of the High Court of Rochefort.

We are hereby contacting you about the child Delphine Robin.

This child was rehospitalized in Nantes at our request for elucidation of a series of symptoms continuing after her long medical journey which led to the removal of a kidney and a final diagnosis of Münchhausen syndrome by proxy.

The child was hospitalized this time for a blood pressure assessment.

A hospitalization in the department with clinical and paraclinical explorations [...] did not confirm the hypothesis of this diagnosis at all. It seems that, at the mother's insistence, the search for a medical diagnosis continued after the last interview we had, which had led to a letter addressed to the children's judge and the doctors concerned.

The question that arises is what to do about the management of this case.

Dr. Gauthier and I have somewhat different views. It is voluntarily that we present here our divergent views. Indeed, they seem to us to testify to what usually happens in the management of these cases: each one has an opinion which can be different, and finally the management cannot be organized with coherence.

As far as I am concerned (Dr. Carrez), I think that the child has already been returned once to this family with a request to the mother not to continue her explorations without strict medical supervision. The time seems to me to be overdue to return the child to her family of origin and I am clearly in favor of a very prolonged separation. I would even ask the questions in the opposite direction. Namely, the problem does not seem to me to be that of a separation or not, but that of a medical and legal error: are we not, in fact, continuing to subject a child to a risk of abuse by leaving her with her parents who have "proven themselves in this area"? Is it not possible to think that

"This child and this family need to be supervised"

the care and the legal supervision until now have been insufficient? Indeed, is there not a dimension of the problem which is situated at the penal level as in the other forms of child abuse because, without any doubt, the Münchhausen syndrome by proxy constitutes a form of child abuse.

Dr. Gauthier believes that a strict medical follow-up can still be tried for a few months, but under the cover of a close psychothera-peutic care of the family.

Finally, the fundamental problem of these mothers who have children on whom they induce a Münchhausen syndrome by proxy, is that of the "cleavage". On the one hand, they have a normal psychic functioning and the contact with them does not let anything show. In depth, on the contrary, their perception of their child remains frankly delirious and induces the multiplication of the symptomatology.

Each of us, as is extremely common in the case of Münchhausen by proxy or child abuse in a more general way, ends up possessing a part of the truth and having the best reasons not to modify the current situation, provided that strict supervision is carried out. However, this must be possible and, for example, medical monitoring must be placed under the authority of the juvenile judge. Otherwise, the global perception of the case escapes us and we cannot carry out a synthesis that would be beneficial to the child.

That is why we are sending today this circular letter to Judge Guinet and to the concerned doctors. Please also find attached an article which gives an overview of the Münchhausen syndrome by proxy.

Indeed, these cases are extremely rare and therefore quite "trapping" for each physician who has to deal with them.

We would like, if possible, to set up a meeting where we would gather all the concerned practitioners as well as the juvenile judge in order to find a coherent way to deal with this child and her family.

I say: "of her family"! Indeed, it seems to me imperative also that a control of the medical follow-up of the siblings of this child can be set up because we know that in certain families, it is several children who are concerned by this maternal madness.

Doctor Carrez and Doctor Gauthier.

Recipients:
- Doctor Florent, Saintes
- Doctor Pelletier, Marennes
- Doctor Brunet, La Rochelle
- Doctor Hacquin, Bourcefranc-le-Chapus

I don't remember this separation that seems to be mentioned by Dr. Carrez and Dr. Gauthier. I just remember being a few days in the department where Dr. Gauthier works, in pediatrics. I was given some basic tests to make sure I was in good physical health, and I actually stayed there for several days. I lived this stay as an umpteenth hospitalization, I believe that not one of the specialists who took care of me at the time explained to me why I was there. However, I would learn a few years later that there had been a question of a separation from my family, so that mother and daughter could be "de-fused". Did I repress this explanation at the time? Or was I really told nothing? In that case, what a mistake, maybe if I had known...

What is clear in my little girl's mind is that I am afraid of being placed in a home; lately I have been hearing a lot about it. I hear the words "juvenile judge", "court"... No one really explains to me what's going on, but I know it's not normal or reassuring.

At school, I am ashamed, I don't want anyone to know anything about what is going on in my home, in my life. I never talk about my worries, the questions that bother me. On the contrary, I try to show others, my friends, the rest of the family, the children of my parents' friends that we are a "normal" family. I try to put on a smile, to look like a happy little girl. But I am deeply sad and anxious, I feel like a loser, ugly, stupid.

I notice it at school, nobody comes to me, nobody is interested in me. The kids often make fun of me, but everything I try to hide, they have to see anyway.

I have a very bad experience in elementary school, my results are frankly pathetic. The handing out of the report cards at the end of each term is wonderfully well thought out by the teachers: they don't bother to take precautions not to show the bad pupils. No, they have a real talent for that. These moments that I experienced from CE2 to CM2 are engraved in my memory. These were more humiliations in my daily life, which started at the beginning of the year: for three years, my teachers placed me at the back of the class, alone at a desk. It must be said that from the beginning of the school year, my mother presented me as a sick, tired child who could not hold back to go to the bathroom, so I had to be allowed to go out during the lessons without being kept waiting. In addition, I was frequently absent from school and quite late.

So I wasn't going to tell anyone now that there was a juvenile judge who was interested in our family.

This period was very difficult for me. My anxieties invade me even more, I repress them, but when I find myself alone in the evening, in my room, they trap me. The questions turn in loop in my head, the fear of dying is always omnipresent. I know that my parents are together while I am in bed: what are they doing? My fears are so strong that I often refuse to go to bed. My parents are annoyed, I have the impression that they do not take me seriously.

"What a comedienne, that one!

The elder one adds a layer, as if he was happy to see me not feeling well.

February 23, 1994
To the attention of the Children's Judge.

Mr. Verdier had indicated to me that a meeting had been held in your offices on February 4, 1994 concerning the child Delphine Robin living in Bourcefranc-le-Chapus.

The case of Delphine was reported to you by Dr Carrez and Dr Gauthier, hospital practitioners in Nantes. The diagnosis of Münchhausen syndrome by proxy had been made in view of the falsification of the medical results by the mother, which had led to the confirmation of various medical and surgical procedures whose validity was not always obvious.

On the day of this meeting, I had made an appointment with Mr. and Mrs. Robin to consider with them a work of care, of prevention of what one can call an induced abuse.

Certainly, Mr. and Mrs. Robin were completely focused on waiting for your judgment and Delphine was particularly tense, anxious, resisting with all her might any separation from her parents.

During this second interview and in the presence of her husband, Mrs. Robin was able to evoke her gesture as a form of anticipatory panic and a provocation to the medical profession to do something for her daughter.

We have mentioned the failure of psychotherapeutic work...

During our meeting, I discussed with Mr. and Mrs. Robin the possibility of family therapy work that could be carried out in Saintes with themselves and their child, subject to a motivating injunction from you; in other words, it would be quite possible for us to carry out this work, provided that it meets your expectations and is fixed by an order from you.

Doctor Florent, child psychiatrist.

According to my research, it is at this time that all this upheaval faded away. We did not see Dr. Florent or Dr. Carrez again. It had been decided to provide educational assistance for twelve months, that's all.

In 2008, I found the man who was in charge of this educational assistance. I got in touch with him by phone, I told him vaguely my story; indeed, he had some memories of my family. He assured me that he thought the accusations about my mother were perhaps exaggerated by the doctors, because he thought we were a close and happy family. My mother seemed devoted, attentive to her daughter. As for me, he had noticed that I was anxious and, as he had some knowledge of sophrology, he tried to help me by this means. I told him the truth about my mother's treatment. I briefly explained to him what I was feeling at that time, what I was refusing to say, what I was trying to hide...

"I didn't know that. I thought maybe the doctors had imagined the worst. I didn't think the situation was that bad. We may have been out of line."

AN ALMOST NORMAL LIFE

The educator came to the house for six months. No one explained to me who he was or why he came regularly. I thought that the surgeon had recommended that my mother make appointments with a sophrologist to try to calm my invasive anxieties. Mom had not given me any instructions on what to do while he was there. I easily accept the different ways he suggests to help me. I don't know that he is an educator or that the judge for children has requested educational assistance. I am convinced that things are back to normal. There is no longer any question of removing me from my home or accusing mom of anything. In fact, I am undergoing far fewer medical investigations.

In September 1995, I continued my studies at the college in the town closest to our home. I arrived in the 6th grade with the gaps I had accumulated during my primary school years. I felt completely lost socially and academically.

My only friend is my mother, but I don't want her to be my friend, I want her to be my mother and accept me as I am: a young girl who can have friends without having her mother always behind her.

As for my average, it is catastrophic in every subject. I still can't do multiplication, division or solve mathematical problems; in

French, I can't do an essay, I don't understand anything, I make a lot of spelling mistakes, conjugation mistakes... It's a total failure. Once again, the teachers don't pay too much attention to all my difficulties, I'm in the back of the class and I wait for time to pass. I'm completely out of touch, I'm just showing up. I am categorized under the same heading as the oldest child who also went to this school and had many behavioral problems.

At home, he still exercises his despotism with the complicity of his mother. I'm fed up, I'm in a hurry to become an adult, to be able to live my life outside this heavy family climate.

Despite the great complicity between Mom and her oldest son, there are also times when I feel like she hates him. She speaks badly to him, she is vulgar When she is angry, it is as if she no longer likes the person she is angry at.

"You are not at home here, you are at my place! You have nothing to say, it is me who commands, it is me who decides!" she sometimes throws us violently.

I am saddened by this, but I don't react, she scares me when she is in this state.

"Why did you get us if we're messing with you?" my older brother sometimes asks him.

When she gets into trouble with him, she sometimes kicks him out of the house. The first time this happened, he was probably about 15 years old. She put all his clothes in garbage bags and threw them out. As much as I hate him, I can't help but think that's an overreaction for a mother.

It is true that he has a difficult behavior to manage. He started drinking and taking drugs at a very young age, he is frequently expelled from school, he lives on the fringe of society. He has a lot of problems with the police because of his associations. He pretends to steal the bikes of the whole family, but I'm sure he sells them to buy his drugs. At night he goes out, he comes home late; I can't sleep until he comes back, I'm afraid he'll come in drunk, drugged and kill us all while we sleep.

If he has become like this, it is perhaps because of her.

"But I raised all three of them the same way, and he took the wrong path," she often says.

She exasperates me, she does not realize her attitude with us. She loves us and rejects us in turn.

My father, at the time, seems to me to be also victim of the authoritarianism of his wife. She reproaches him more and more, he never answers. I boil internally. I want to defend him, he does not deserve to be put down. But I don't contradict her, because I know that her son will side with mom. He can't stand it when I speak badly, when I answer back, he always wants me to keep quiet, he doesn't hesitate to correct me, or to make fun of me. I feel humiliated, but I don't want it to show, so I take refuge in my room to cry.

Sometimes I feel like I'm overreacting to what's going on at home, that I'm imagining things, that maybe it's not better at home. But I really feel that this is not normal. I don't always feel safe in my family.

Not surprisingly, I repeated my 6th grade year. My two years of delay complicated my relationships with my classmates more and more. I lost the ones I had before, and the new ones were still children when I was starting to enter adolescence.

During this year, I go with my class to a job fair. I stopped in front of a stand that presented the advantages of a work-study program. The establishment presented was a private school, and therefore paying. Knowing my parents' financial worries, I had little hope. I decided to talk to my mother about it anyway.

She agreed to let us visit the premises, meet the director and get information on the payment of school fees in this establishment. The only drawback is that you have to pass your 5th grade class to get in. So I had to work hard. A year and a half! I'm hanging on to that prospect.

Mom, on the other hand, is slowly starting to worry about my kidney and my diabetes again. She starts checking my blood sugar several times a day, at the same time as she checks hers.

March 1997
To the attention of Dr. Brunet, nephrologist, La Rochelle Hospital.

I had the opportunity to see in consultation one of your patients, Miss Delphine Robin, followed by your care for a vesico-ureteral reflux on a single kidney.

The questioning here reveals the notion of a high family penetrance of non-insulin-dependent diabetes (mother, maternal aunt and uncle, maternal grandparents).

Repeated capillary blood glucose checks were performed by Ms. Robin's mother for this purpose and may have shown suspicious fasting blood glucose values.

Based on these data, I suggest that you perform an oral glucose tolerance test in order to determine the exact glycemic status and that you follow a certain number of dietary measures, including the exclusion of fast sugars and an approximate quantification of slow and semi-slow sugars, in order to limit the subsequent risks of the emergence of true diabetes mellitus.

Dr. Bacle, diabetologist.

March 1997
To the attention of Dr. Brunet, nephrologist, La Rochelle Hospital.

Delphine Robin's oral glucose tolerance test was completely normal.
The fasting blood glucose measured at two-hour intervals is strictly normal.

For the time being, there is no true diabetes mellitus or even glucose intolerance, but weight monitoring and compliance with the previously recommended dietary measures are still required.

Dr. Bacle, diabetologist.

My mother no longer talks to me about diabetes and I don't take any special dietary precautions.

A DIFFICULT EMANCIPATION

I passed! I passed my 5th grade class. One more year and I will change schools. It's barely September and I'm already starting to think about the next school year. I see it as a real opportunity for growth. There are fewer students and since it is a private school, maybe the teachers are more invested in their work and will take time with me. And maybe there will be other students in my school situation.

I will also need a means of transportation for my internships: my mother has already told me that it is out of the question for her to go back and forth to take me to my work place. I would need a scooter, but I know that my parents will not have the financial means to offer it to me.

I then remember a sum of money that was paid to me on an account, blocked until my majority. Indeed, following the car accident of December 1990, my mother started a procedure against the person who would have been responsible. She had called a lawyer, and I had been examined by an expert doctor to judge the real consequences of this accident. Perhaps I had been told at the time the amount of money that was due to me at the end of this procedure, but that was the least of my worries.

Today, on the contrary, it is becoming my major concern. I ask mom to make an appointment with the guardianship judge who is in charge of my file to try to get the money needed to buy a scooter.

She accompanied me to the meeting. I explain my project, my wish to continue my education in a private school, in alternation, and my need for a means of transportation.

"That's not possible, your mother took the whole amount."

I am in shock. So much so that I don't remember if the judge gave me the amount I should have had at that time.

"It is mandatory that your mother pay back this amount of money before you come of age."

I was 14 years old at the time. He established a monthly debt repayment plan. My mother seems to agree, she gives her word to the judge that she will pay back the money, we sign a document proving her commitment.

We must review this judge in one year to report on the progress of the reimbursement.

But as soon as we left the judge's office, my mother explained to me that she would not be able to give me the money back, as the means of the household did not allow it, especially as the private school I wanted to go to was expensive. She asks me to write a letter to the judge for our next appointment, explaining that it is not possible for my parents to assume the repayment of this debt.

"What did you use that money for?

- I asked for advances to cover the expenses of your hospitalizations. I always slept in a hotel the first night, gave you gifts when you came back It was for you that I did all this!"

But I didn't like his gifts, I felt like I was being spoiled because I was going to die soon. I would have preferred that the money stayed where it was and that I could use it today. My heart is tight and I'm angry, but once again I'm holding back and building up resentment.

"Ask your grandfather to buy you a scooter. He can afford it and you are his 'little darling'," she suggests.

I hate to ask for money, I don't want to be like him, begging for money from others, I want to be on my own.

"Ask him, you."

After all, it's partly because of her that we're in this situation. She knows no shame and has the art and manner to present things well. She accepts to solicit her father.

"Fine, but let's not talk about this story again. And your father doesn't need to know."

I soon get my brand new and shiny scooter. I'm thrilled, I finally have some independence.

I began to make friends with a few people, acquaintances of my brother Paul who attended the same college as me. We got into the habit of meeting in a bar in our "village" on Wednesday afternoons, after school.

Mom blames me for changing, she doesn't approve of me going out when I'm only 14. I have the feeling that she doesn't appreciate that I don't spend my free time with her anymore.

Is this why, after she calmed down after the appearance before the judge of the children because of the falsification of my biological results and the absence of negative results regarding my diabetes, she suddenly starts again in the medical investigations? To try to get me back under her thumb, to become the center of all my attention again?

One month after the beginning of the school year, following a consultation at Dr. Brunet's office in La Rochelle, because I was complaining from time to time of slight pain in my right kidney, she called Dr. Brissaud to alert him and to mention the possibility of a J-tube, mentioned by the nephrologist. He answered her by mail:

Concerning Delphine, I think that if the painful symptomatology is still present, it will be necessary to consider the installation of a double J catheter.

This can be done during a day hospital stay, which means that Delphine will have to arrive one morning to be seen by the anesthesiologists, then have a small anesthesia and she can leave in the evening for your home.

It would be desirable to do this during the school vacations, i.e. next Thursday, October 30.

So Mom takes charge and seems determined. I'm not too thrilled with the idea, even though Mom tries to convince me by assuring me that I won't be hospitalized.

I wasn't worried about the pain in my right side. Why did I have to tell my mother? She didn't bother me anymore with all these medical questions, I didn't imagine that she would start the whole infernal machine again. I have the feeling that I have trapped myself, I am terribly angry with myself. She gave me her instructions before meeting Dr. Brissaud, but I am not 9 years old anymore, I don't want to listen to her. I decide to remain moderate at the time of the auscultation.

During the whole consultation with Dr. Brissaud, whom I have not seen since 1992, I feel guilty and embarrassed. He looks me straight in the eyes, I think he believes I am lying to him. He explains to me that it is perhaps normal that I feel some pain because of the operation carried out in October 1991 on my only kidney, but that it is not serious.

"I don't see the point of going back to that kidney."

He refused to put in the double J catheter that was initially planned. The consultation was finally quick, and I am relieved.

However, I understand that my mother is not going to listen to her and that she will start her investigations again. She decided to have me followed up twice a year, which meant a CT scan with iodine injection, an ECBU, a blood test, and a consultation with Dr. Brunet.

I continue to escape from his grip and from my family life by going out in the evenings and on weekends with the friends I've managed to make. I am only 15 years old, but I go to discos, I start to smoke, to drink in a sometimes immoderate way. I know I'm not taking care of myself, but I feel in control of my life - for the first time.

My mother does not like my behavior at all.

"You have changed. Will you always be my little Nénette?" she often asks me.

"Yes."

But no, I don't want to remain her "little Nénette". She gets on my nerves more and more.

September 1998

To Dr. Brissaud, urologist, Nantes University Hospital.

You are going to see the young Delphine Robin, whom you know well, and whose general condition is perfectly fine, except for persistent lumbar pain on the right side as soon as the bladder is in replenishment.

The growth in weight and height was quite correct.

There is no headache. Blood pressure is normal.

Biologically, everything is normal.

There is no disorder of the calcemia or phosphoremia. A very small amount of glucosuria persisted. Proteinuria and urinary ionogram are correct. The last ECBU performed showed the presence of Escherichia coli *and* Staphylococcus aureus, *although there were no clinical signs of urinary infection.*

This result does not surprise me since Delphine drinks relatively little. Considering the antibiogram, I simply proposed a treatment with Noroxin.

In conclusion, Delphine's only problem is the persistence of back pain related to a bladder emptying that is perhaps not frequent enough and, in this sense, I insisted to Delphine that she could empty her bladder as frequently as possible.

Doctor Brunet, nephrologist, La Rochelle Hospital.

Of course, the results of the ECBU are suspect since my mother continues to do them without using the sterile tube provided. As for drinking water, I'm so mad I'm breaking the rules. Why does he believe Mom when she tells him this? Why doesn't he listen to me?

The good news is that I'm entering the private school I wanted to go to, to do a 4th and 3rd technological sandwich course, which I think will be more adapted to my level than a normal school course. The school is a bit far from home, so I have to be a boarder, but that doesn't bother me, quite the contrary.

The school director and my mother think that I could do the internships planned in retirement homes or in hospital services, in geriatrics. I have absolutely no desire to do so and make this known. The director immediately classified me as stubborn and rebellious. Anyway, from now on, I don't want anyone to decide for me.

I ended up getting what I wanted: to work with children.

I met the person in charge of a parental day care center on the island of Oléron. I get along well with her and the contact is good with the rest of the team. But I feel like a little girl damaged by life, who has just failed here, I don't have confidence in myself. I have a hard time seeing myself as a young teenager going through the motions of "normal" life and still being happy. What confuses me is that I am well aware of how I feel, but I don't know why. And I don't want the people I work with at the daycare center to know that I'm not comfortable in my own skin.

I would like to do all my weeks of internship in this nursery, I don't want to go anywhere else. The director likes me, it warms my heart to be appreciated by someone and for who I am. I feel useful, important for what I do - not for my illness. The little girl I was disappears here, nobody knows her, nobody knows. So I make sure to keep Mom away from this place that belongs only to me; if she were to meet a member of the nursery staff, I know she would talk about the child who was seriously ill and is still fragile. And I know I would be looked at differently.

However, during this year of alternation, I am obliged to do internships in other places. I am forced to go to a school canteen, a hospital crèche and another parent's crèche in another town.

November 1998
To Dr. Brunet, nephrologist and Dr. Hacquin, attending physician.

I saw Delphine Robin, 15 years old, in consultation, whom I had not seen since 1992 [sic].

This girl has two problems.

The first is a left lumbar scar with a costal diastasis. Delphine asked for a cosmetic repair that we can do without any problem, knowing that it is not only a skin problem but also a costal problem that needs to be resolved at the same time.

The second one is that of lumbar pain on the right side which appears when the bladder is full. In fact, as Delphine had initially been operated on in La Rochelle with an anti-reflux device according to Cohen, there is obviously a small obstructive syndrome at the level of her uretero-bladder junction, which means that there is no longer any reflux when the bladder is full and that there is retention of urine in the right upper urinary tract. This explains perfectly the pain that Delphine has in the right lumbar region, without the kidney suffering abnormally for the moment. There is no medical treatment, and I did not write a prescription, nor did I prescribe Di-Antalvic or Spasfon, which obviously do not help. I explained to Delphine that the situation was quite stable for the moment on a nephrological and urological level and that I had to deal with these pains, even if I had to urinate a little more often than my girlfriends, I would certainly have to intervene again at the level of this right uretero-vesical junction only if the situation, on a renal level, were to really deteriorate.

One of the periods of risk for Delphine will certainly be that of a possible pregnancy, since she carries a single kidney on her right side. I have informed Delphine, face to face, of this problem, so that she can be taken care of at that time.

Here is the last information about Delphine which does not seem to me very complicated.

Regarding the left lumbar parietal problem, I told Delphine that I was at her disposal and that it would not cost her much, since I would do it myself in a public hospital.

Doctor Brissaud, urologist, Nantes University Hospital.

I really have the feeling, at the time of this consultation, that Mr. Brissaud is tired of seeing us. I wonder what he thinks after all that has happened, but I don't dare talk about it, I promised mom. So I concentrate on my scar problem. I really want to have reconstructive surgery. I'm so self-conscious that I only wear one-piece bathing suits so it doesn't show. But the hospitalization, the operating room and the anesthesia scare me a lot, I don't want to go through that again.

As for his explanations for the pregnancy, I let him give them to me, but I don't want to hear them; I know that I will be in great shape, even more than someone who has both kidneys. I don't want any special follow-up, I want to be taken care of like a "normal" person.

I kept telling myself, "When I grow up, I can choose to be like everyone else. I'm tired of being different because of my health concerns.

Anyway, at the moment my love life is catastrophic. I started flirting shyly with a boy and told a girl in my class who lives in the same village as me. One weekend, as soon as I passed the door of the family house, my mother fell on me and slapped me. I crouched down in a corner of the kitchen, protecting my face with my arms. She strikes again and insults me:

"Fuck! Bitch! Gosh, I never thought my daughter would give herself to the first guy!"

I hate my mother, I hate that girl I told about my crush and she reported it to my mother. What could she bring back anyway? Nothing had happened, nothing will happen with him: for a long time, I didn't have a boyfriend, I couldn't do it, I was too shy, too shy.

Nevertheless, this year is going pretty well for me; I don't have any other medical investigations and except for the weekends when I have to go home, I am completely free to move around and gain more and more autonomy between courses - and then there is the scooter.

I make new friends, who assure me that my scar is not so ugly, we go out together, I lie to my mother who still doesn't appreciate the liberties I take, but I don't leave her the choice. I sleep here and there, I go to bars, discos, I go on vacations... It's an extremely beneficial period for me, which allows me to get away from my mother, but also to realize, while the girls I date are about the same age as me, that I feel much younger than them and don't allow myself certain things that they do quite naturally, such as dating boys.

I understand that I did not grow up the same way and that I am also suffering the consequences of this emotionally.

WHEN THE CHILD VICTIM RESURFACES

My level improved a bit, and I entered 3rd grade.

I plan to stay in the same school to continue in my second and final year of vocational studies in order to obtain a BEPA in personal services, and eventually to continue my studies in the early childhood sector. But just the idea that I would always have to oppose the director's and my mother's wishes regarding my professional future scares me. So I'm thinking of going to another private high school that offers the work-study program I want in order to escape their intransigent authority.

In the meantime, this last year has to go.

I would like to return to the crèche on the island of Oleron where I still feel so good and where I am very involved.

But during the year, the situation became really difficult. I was forced to go to a local hospital for an internship in the geriatric medicine department: my mother and the director agreed without asking my opinion.

I hold back my rage, but I already know that I won't be able to stay there for the whole period of time that is imposed on me.

I asked, initially, to accompany the team in charge of the maintenance of the premises, it is out of the question for me to accompany the care team.

When I arrived the first morning, I was filled with apprehension. I feel so oppressed that as soon as I get there, I want to run away. I force myself, at least to stay for one day. I stay away all morning, I don't talk to the people who are supervising me and I make it clear right away that this internship has been imposed on me and that I don't want to be here. This admission does not make my integration easier, I am well aware of it, but I don't care.

I am asked to take charge of a sector of rooms for maintenance. I enter the room of a gentleman I barely dare to look at. I briefly perform my duties, thinking that once I am done, I will leave this place and not return.

I left the hospital without telling anyone, took my scooter and went home. Of course, my mother reproaches me for my act and, as usual, she doesn't care about my justifications, she has the art and the way to make me doubt my seriousness and my capacity to assert the choices which are good for me. As for the director of the school, I also know that this will not go down well, she will note in my file how stubborn and rebellious I am. This is my professional career: how can they afford to judge me and impose their will on me when I simply know what I want?

I was summoned to the director's office with my mother to discuss my behavior. The decision was made to send me on an internship in a retirement home. The place chosen was a religious retirement home on the island of Oleron, where Mom knew someone who worked there. I wanted to run away during the whole interview, I wanted to scream to be left alone.

Once again, as soon as I get there, I run away from this place that frightens and terrorizes me. I don't know why, but I can't do it.

As my mother worked in a retirement home in the town where we lived, she asked for a place for me; as I categorically refused to take care of the elderly, I joined the team of catering agents. As it went well, I stayed there for two months, alternating with the weeks at school.

Nevertheless, I will have to do an internship with elderly people before the end of my 3rd year. I decide to undertake it in the establishment where my mother works. If I am with her, she will spare me; as I dread caring for people, I could be satisfied with serving breakfast, making the beds, cleaning...

I don't like what I see, what I hear, what happens there. Nobody reacts; inside I am revolted. Mom is mean to some of the older people; of course, she carefully chooses her tormentors: people who are not in their right mind anymore. She mocks, she humiliates; she is never alone, there are always two of them.

Today, I am disconcerted, I realize the seriousness of these actions. How could I have stood by and done nothing? Just like when I was subjected to Mom's delusional actions? Who am I, what has she done to me that I am able to keep my emotions and feelings bottled up? Why don't I assert myself?

So I remained a little girl victim?

In any case, it seems that everyone is trying to keep me in this position.

In January, during my check-ups and consultation with the nephrologist in La Rochelle, the subject of the double catheter came up again: my pain persisted, my mother and Dr. Brunet remained convinced that this was the solution to the problem.

This time, Dr. Brissaud agreed to do it. Why does he decide to perform this operation when some time before he seemed to think we were lying and had explained to me that the operation was not advised on my single kidney? Is he doing this because he is tired of our insistence? At least my mother's? Or is he really doing this to ease the pain?

No matter what the reasons are, I don't want to go back to the operating room, be put to sleep there and be hospitalized again, even for a day. I'm just starting to enjoy life, go out, have friends, be independent, spend time without thinking about all my "health" problems that everyone I know now ignores.

I don't explain to them that I don't agree, but I know, even before it is placed on me, that I will very quickly ask to have it

When the child victim resurfaces

removed. I don't know what reason I will give but I would like them to understand that I want to be left alone, that I prefer to be in pain from time to time rather than have a "thing" inside my body and undergo all these exams and consultations again.

This is the first time since 1992 that I am hospitalized in Nantes. I am not in the usual children's room. It is normal, I have grown up, but it would have been comforting to be back in my old room.

In the morning, before going to the operating room, I am always so terrified. The same goes for when I come back. But this time I can go home right away. But my kidney really hurts and when I go to the bathroom, all I see is blood. I'm afraid that if I go home and anything happens to me, there's nothing anyone can do. I would rather stay overnight, go home when the pain and blood have stopped. The nurse doesn't understand why I don't want to leave, why I am afraid.

"Please ask Dr. Brissaud if it's normal for my kidney to hurt and for me to urinate blood!"

My request seems to make her angry.

"Dr. Brissaud has gone home."

I'm really sorry to be a pain in the ass, but I think I need some reassurance. So I stay one night.

February 2000
To the attention of Dr. Brunet, nephrologist, La Rochelle Hospital.

I took over at the urological clinic of the CHU of Nantes Delphine Robin.

So I decided to have a double J catheter placed to see if all this drainage would decrease her pain.

I therefore intervened on Thursday, February 10. I was able to mount a probe endoscopically without too much trouble.

Afterwards, the urine remained somewhat hematuric, but there was nothing alarming.

Because of this less hematuric urine, Mrs. Robin mother wanted to leave the ward. She and her daughter returned home on February 11, 2000.

I will leave the probe in place for two months and will check with Delphine at that time.

Doctor Brissaud, urologist, Nantes University Hospital.

So we see him again in April. I still feel guilty and uncomfortable around him. I find it very regrettable that I came back to see him after everything that happened when I was 9 years old. And just as my mother didn't want us to talk about the two doctors in Nantes, I didn't want them to talk about my kidney anymore.

My mother did not give me any instructions before the examination. So, I want to explain to Dr. Brissaud that the probe is bothering me, that it has to be removed and that I am fine. I want to be able to leave here very quickly. But I don't dare. However, I feel that he is listening to me, that he is attentive to what I want. But I can't express it to him, I prefer to let mom speak. When he asks me questions, I just answer with insecure nods. I am not able to say what I think about this situation. Yet, I would have "a billion" questions to ask him. They keep popping into my head when I'm alone but I prefer to stay in my confusion. I consider myself a liar, a kid who wants to be taken care of, and my mother would not like it if she knew that I had doubts about all the symptoms we were talking about. Not to mention that Dr. Brissaud would still be suspicious of her. What image does he have of my mother? I prefer to remain the little girl I have always been in front of all these doctors.

To think that I didn't want this damn probe at all! How ironic! My mother is back to worrying about my kidney and getting her grip even though I feel fine. But she's come to terms with the fact that I'm sick, and the more I move away and gain independence, the more she insists.

Taming the shy teenager

During this year, Damien is getting closer and closer to me. I'm not very comfortable with this; he's older than me and I have no idea how to deal with boys. But I like his company: he is interested in me, he is nice. I accept his friendship and share it, but I don't ask for more. I'm afraid our relationship will go further.

He and I had known each other for a long time; we regularly met at the same parties and we got along very well. But I didn't think he wanted more. I'm beginning to understand him now. And when he makes it clear that he wants something else from our relationship, I refuse. Damien accepts that the fierce little girl stays in her shell and continues to see me and be close to me despite everything.

However, I gradually extracted myself from the timid child. When I saw Dr. Brunet again in La Rochelle in June, I claimed that the catheter was bothering me so that it could finally be removed. But the nephrologist claimed that it was bothering me because it was blocked. I insisted that it should be removed and not put in another one, but he stuck to his guns: "It's clogged, better change it. Dr. Brunet never takes my word for it, he only listens to my mother. I am exasperated and ready to stick to my guns this time. I let Dr. Brissaud change my catheter as the nephrologist had suggested, but contacted him again a few days later. I know he listens to me and can make it stop.

June 29, 2000
To the attention of Dr. Brunet, nephrologist, La Rochelle Hospital.

I saw Delphine Robin again in consultation.

Back pain recurred while a double J catheter was in place in the right kidney. This catheter was perfectly in place, both in the kidney and in the bladder.

We can therefore clear the right kidney of any pathology because of the persistence of pain under a double J probe, non-functional and obstructive.

Under these conditions, I leave Delphine alone and I ask her to continue her renal surveillance with Dr. Brunet, nephrologist in La Rochelle.

Doctor Brissaud, urologist, Nantes University Hospital.

I will finally be able to regain the peace and quiet I had recently begun to enjoy. I promise myself not to talk about pain to my mother anymore. I don't want to see Mr. Brissaud again. I don't want to go to a scanner twice a year, I don't want to go to the nephrologist twice a year. I accept a simple ultrasound, a blood test and the consultation with the nephrologist only once a year.

There is no way I am going to let anyone talk about my kidney anymore. I want to be well now and I know I am! Mr. Brissaud says so and I want to believe him.

I am freeing myself more and more, I see Damien very regularly, to the point of abandoning my friends. We go out one on one, I feel better and better in his company and I get closer to him. He sometimes brings me back to the front of the house. Every time my parents see him dropping me off, they tell me that he is not a nice person.

I don't care, I feel good with him, I let myself go little by little, I accept that he is more tender, that he takes me in his arms. The little girl lets herself be tamed step by step.

Summer arrives, and our relationship takes another turn, friendship gives way to a slightly more serious relationship. I tell myself that this is finally pleasant. But I don't consider at this moment that our story is serious. I consider that we are not part of the same world; his friends and mine are very different, as well as the outings we each do on our own. However, as time goes by, I realize that he is not quite like his friends, whom he is beginning to see less and less. To the point that I am getting more and more attached to him.

My parents don't know anything about our relationship; I sleep at his place - he still lives with his mother - and come home early in the morning, as if I were coming back from a party with my girlfriends so they wouldn't suspect anything.

But Mom eventually suspects something. She tries to make me believe that she accepts this relationship, but doesn't hesitate to make a remark at the slightest opportunity.

"He's a thug, he's been hanging out on the streets at a very young age, he's a drug addict, like your brother. You are really not well my poor girl!"

She is jealous of Damien, but also jealous of Damien's mother because she thinks I love her more than my own mother! She especially hates it when I move away from her, when her authority no longer works on me. I get a certain pleasure out of it, I'm happy to oppose her opinion, and it doesn't matter if she's right in the end.

Sometimes, with her oldest son, she asks me questions about my relationship with Damien.

"How is it possible that you have a boyfriend when you are always prudish at home?"

Of course I hide in front of my elder, what does he think? He exasperates me, I hate him.

"I know Damien better than you, he won't stay with you very long. You are not a girl for him," he throws at me.

As always, I answer him in a very vulgar and aggressive way.

I end up spending my vacations at Damien's to escape their humiliation. I only come home to do my laundry. I am alone at his mother's during the day, both of them work. In the afternoons, I go to the beach, I come back after Damien's work. I am accepted and appreciated by his family, simple and kind. I remained a little reserved at first. I observe this family, so different from mine. I avoid talking about my parents and my brothers; if I am asked questions, I don't say what I really think, I give the best possible image of my family. This has always been my way of hiding this painful daily life that my mother and her son make me live.

Damien doesn't think much of my mother, he agrees to come to my house when necessary, for a meal, but only to please me and because he likes my father in spite of everything.

My parents and my brother Paul are taking advantage of the summer to go to Germany, on a trip organized by the firemen's association. So I have the house with Damien for a week. Only black point, my elder brother plans to come to make a "party". But I hope that he will change his mind, as mom has forbidden him to bring friends home.

But on the first night, he shows up with all his buddies. They live in trucks, don't work, take drugs, spend their time on the road. They push all the furniture in the living room, invade the place with their sound equipment. I can't say anything, he dominates me.

The next morning, they are all sprawled on the couch or on the floor, sleeping or comatose. The house is in a deplorable state, I want to scream, to throw them all out, but once again my brother's reaction scares me. I especially don't want to take a slap in front of Damien. We leave the place during the day. Damien does not talk to me about what has just happened. I think that he does not appreciate the marginal behavior of my elder brother; it is a way of life that he knew himself at one time and from which he perhaps wanted to escape by our history.

When I tell my parents about these events on their return, it does not provoke any particular reaction; even if my father does not like it, he does not say anything, he seems blasé by his son's behavior.

Yet I remember an argument between them, in which Dad grabbed his son, held him against the front door, his fist ready to punch him in the face.

"Go ahead and hit me if you have any balls," his son yelled at him.

Even if I hate him, I think that this drift, this way of harming himself and those around him is the consequence of our childhood: this mother who rejects us and then makes us dependent on her without our knowing it. All the attention that was given to me, how did my brothers experience it? They would have good reason to hate me after all; our mother's attention was mostly focused on me and led to the compassion of everyone around us for this sick little girl. So what was their part?

THE HOLD ON THE FATHER

After this liberating and emancipating year, I will enter in September the private high school I chose, in Jarnac, in the Charente, where I will prepare my BEPA service to people during two years. I will be a boarder and will have to go there by train.

This prospect makes me a little sad: I won't see Damien for a week. We make an arrangement with my father: he takes me to the station on Monday morning, while Damien picks me up on Friday evening. The weeks of school seem long to me, we communicate by SMS and we call each other.

I have to do several internships in different places. I'm going back to the crèche on the island of Oléron. I am always so happy to work there, the team is always so pleasant and the contact with the children is good. I feel fulfilled, I am swimming in happiness. During the three weeks that I had to work elsewhere, I decided to return to the retirement home where my mother worked; I was much less apprehensive and I realized that I got along well with the elderly; I liked talking with them and I realized that they appreciated that we took the time to stay close to them and to listen to them. However, I still don't feel capable of doing the care. I feel a certain compassion for these people who did not choose to be there, I feel that they have lost the notions they may have had during their "active" life. They are completely subservient to the caregivers.

On the school level, it was a rather positive year and it went well. I also obtained my driver's license after several attempts.

On the other hand, on the family level, the year will be marked by an event that will leave extremely significant and disturbing traces.

In the summer of 2001, my parents had a car accident while on vacation at my maternal grandfather's house in Arcachon.

The car had to be cut up to evacuate my father whose left leg was injured. He was taken by the firemen to the nearest hospital. My mother only has a few bruises.

She is going to make our lives hell while dad is in hospital. Damien and I are at her mercy, we have to go with her wherever and whenever she wants. If we have the misfortune to refuse, she puts so much pressure on us that we are forced to give in anyway.

"You can't deny your parent anything. And with everything I've done for you, this is how you thank me? So you don't love me, I can't count on you?

I understand better how she was always able to get what she wanted.

She is very worried about the state of dad's leg: it hurts too much, the pain is not sufficiently relieved, the operation must have been done badly, the healing is too long, his leg is still too swollen. She keeps asking him if his leg hurts, she keeps repeating that it is not normal.

I am a spectator of all this energy that she deploys for dad, I am boiling, I feel that she is starting again: she is going to exaggerate the symptoms that dad presents, to convince him that he suffers, that the operation is failed, that it is necessary to start again... However, I do not make the association at that time with what I myself lived.

I feel like my dad is being brainwashed, she keeps telling him the same things over and over again and says that the people you think are friends aren't, because they don't come to see him often enough for her taste.

She also seems determined to do everything possible to get the insurance company of the person who caused the accident to pay them a fairly large sum of money. For example, she asks my father to take a cane to appointments with the medical expert, even though he never uses it the rest of the time.

The climate at home is unbearable, this event takes a hallucinating extent, my mother exhausts me psychically. I am worn out. I can't take it anymore, but I keep quiet so that she doesn't try to convince me at all costs that all her efforts are for Dad's sake.

He ends up letting her decide for him. She takes him to a clinic where she knows the orthopedic surgeon:

"He's good, he'll fix the other good-for-nothing's crap."

At the same time, she decides to hire a lawyer to file a complaint against the first surgeon who "botched" the operation. She claims that they did it too late, that Dad will have after-effects. The director did not want to worry the surgeon about this case and told my mother that they would work it out with the hospital's insurance: she obtained compensation.

But this is not enough for her, she regularly presses Dad, reminding him of the after-effects of the first operation:

"You'll never be able to go back to work, my poor Alain!"

He finds himself on sick leave for a long period of time, they stop paying the monthly payments on the house loan thanks to the death and disability insurance linked to the loan, while the insurance company of the driver who caused the accident pays a very good compensation.

It's all very convenient, I think she's going to be able to pay back all her debts, but no, she spends this money indiscriminately, without caring about the people she owes money to. I feel ashamed when I meet our creditors, they must think we are a bad family, petty and unpleasant.

Finally, in the long run, we got used to this new life: dad doesn't work anymore, mom is working hard to have him recognized as unfit. He obtained a percentage of handicap, a pension from the CAF and a handicap card from the COTOREP.

I don't recognize him anymore. He has put on weight, he has no social life, no professional activity, he seems bitter. He is in admiration of everything his wife does.

I realize that she is ready to devastate everything in her path to achieve her goals.

Towards independence

My final year of vocational school is going well: I continue to see Damien on weekends, my mother leaves me in peace with my health problems and, this year, I can do all my internships at the crèche: this will be taken into account in the final exam, the BEPA.

I'm pretty confident: I want to graduate, I want to quit school, I want to find a job and settle down with Damien. However, I would like to pass my high school diploma, but I know that I am unable to do so because I am behind in my schooling, and I want to leave home, live my life, away from my mother.

After passing the exam, I applied for the summer for a position as a leader in a leisure center; I don't have the BAFA, but as I have experience in a nursery, I was accepted. So I will work there for two months. I had the best summer of my life. I work ten hours a day, five days a week, but I really don't feel like I'm working: the kids are great, the counselors are great, I feel really good around them. And, apparently, the feeling is mutual, because at the end of the season, I was offered a replacement in September until the end of the All Saints' vacation.

Once this period was over, my only activity was baby-sitting. So I decided to take the nursery assistant exam, hoping to find a job in a nursery more easily.

I received the results in November 2002: I did not pass the competition. So I started looking for a job in any field. It was the price to pay for being together with Damien! I answer an ad for cosmetic products, making a good effort to get a job: it will be a new experience. I also wrote to the hospital in Saintes, thinking that I might be offered a job in pediatrics as an animator, even though I didn't really believe it.

In December, while I was babysitting a 3 year old boy, my cell phone rang: it was the hospital in Saintes, a manager from the geriatric department asked me if I could go to an interview the next day. It was a big disappointment, everything but that! However, I accept. I want a job, I am offered one, I am not going to refuse. I think back to that principal at school who kept telling me that there would always be work with the elderly, as opposed to the early childhood field. Was she really right?

I feel uncomfortable during the interview, I feel like the little girl from before, who doesn't dare to assert her thoughts, her choices, to put herself forward.

However, some time later, the hospital in Saintes called me back, asking me to come back to visit the geriatric department and sign my contract for a trial period.

I started in January 2003. At the time of taking up my post, I am apprehensive, I am afraid of not being able to contain myself and, as during my training course, to flee. However, I don't have to, it's an opportunity to become autonomous with Damien. It's an opportunity to cut the cord with mom. So I keep in mind to stay a few months in Saintes; then, when summer comes, I will go back to the leisure center for a season.

Finally my first day goes well. I am the youngest in the department and a bit reserved, but my colleagues welcome me warmly. They tenderly call me "the baby of the department". I feel comfortable with them; without realizing it right away, I put myself in the shoes of the little girl I once was. I let myself be pampered, pampered, mothered.

I am back to the relational contact I had with the elderly during my last internship. That's what I like best, talking with patients and their families.

However, I am taking it upon myself to do the *nursing* care; I still hate it, but I don't want to disappoint my colleagues or have my contract broken. The more the weeks go by, the more I give up the idea of leaving my job. I feel good, I have found "a nice little family. I don't tell them much about myself and when they ask me about my family, I defend the image of perfect happiness. In my mother's eyes, this is the definition of our relationship: complicity and closeness. I see her as a possessive, manipulative, lying, depressive, exuberant mother with no personality of her own. I hold up two of my colleagues as models: loving but not excessive, sincere, fair and discreet. This is the mother I would have liked to have.

Two months after my hiring, I finally start the steps to settle down with Damien... who is not necessarily in a hurry. Of course, my mother gets involved, she follows me in my search for an apartment, convinced that I am happy and that I need her for these steps. I don't dare tell her that I would rather do them with Damien. I don't know how he feels about my mother's intrusion. I feel like I'm shutting him out and I don't like it. He doesn't talk to me about anything, he doesn't show any displeasure. I assume that he doesn't mind; maybe he thinks I like involving my mother and doesn't dare to tell me, so as not to "upset" me.

After we moved in, Mom is still pretty intrusive. She still avoids coming on weekends; I can see that she is trying to respect our privacy, but it seems to me that it is difficult for her.

Farewell grandfather

Since my grandmother passed away, my grandfather has been living with an aunt of my mother's whom we call "Aunt-Nine", who herself lost her husband a few years before. For as long as I can remember, I have hated this woman; there is a certain malice in her eyes, and I feel that she is only interested in my grandfather's money, that she is using him. My mother has no affection for her either; she sees her as taking the place of my grandmother, which I think is true. At one point, she even had a falling out with her, to the point of not seeing her father for a while. She explained to me that her aunt had abandoned her four children when they were small, preferring to chase men rather than raise them. She called her a "whore", declared that "only the train had not passed over her." She gradually calmed down and reconnected with my grandfather and Aunt-Nine.

While they were living in Arcachon until then, they decided to come back to live near mom in 2003. Very quickly, I realized that my grandfather was unhappy with Aunt-Nine. He doesn't talk much, he seems unable to make a decision, he looks like an automaton. I can't help but compare Aunt-Nine to Mom: manipulative, calculating All those years of silence when I resigned myself to repressing any judgment about Mom taught me to recognize the taste of undetectable poison.

I decide to talk to my mother anyway, she listens to me and seems to agree with the description I give her of my grandfather. I wait for her to act, maybe she will find a solution to get my grandfather out of the clutches of this "witch".

Some time later, Mom received a phone call in the middle of the night: Aunt-Nine tells her that my grandfather has fallen while trying to go to the bathroom, and she needs help to get him up. He was taken to the hospital. We learn that the aunt tried to get him up by herself by pulling him by the arm.

Following this incident, my mother arranged to have him placed in the nursing home where she works. Knowing what goes on there, the idea makes my blood run cold. But it seems to be the only way to get him away from Auntie-Nine. She and my mother are still fighting about the placement. Her aunt doesn't like the decision because she won't get my grandfather's pension anymore. Money is all she cares about!

I go to see him every day, at lunchtime or after my working hours. My mother also comes to see him when she is not working. I am amazed at her kindness, she takes care of her father, she is gentle and caring without expecting anything in return. Does she do it to please me? She knows how much I love my grandfather. Or has she changed? She doesn't try to shape his thoughts and cares about his well-being while keeping the right distance. Just as I wish she had done with me.

I feel that he is happy when we are together. He confides in me, "I'm like a rooster," and he talks to me a lot. He tells me episodes of his daily life with Aunt-Nine. I discover with horror, and as I suspected, that she mistreated him. He didn't dare tell her anything. I am revolted. How could she do this? Why didn't I do anything? I remember that when I went to their house on vacation in Arcachon, she wrote down the result of my grandfather's blood sugar test in two notebooks: one where she indicated the right number and a second one where she wrote down a result that would not worry the diabetologist during the consultations. Aunt-Nine doesn't have a license and she was afraid that the doctors would make my grandfather stop driving if his health wasn't good! Again, the little girl was stronger than me at the time. She is now making up for it in any way she can.

We are planning a trip to the beach with my mother and grandfather. But when we come to pick him up, he tells us that he is tired and his legs hurt. So we decide to postpone the walk and stay with him until dinner before taking him back to his room and helping him to bed. I go back home in peace, I see how happy he is and I am very happy.

The next day, while I was busy in a patient's room with a colleague, my boss came to tell me that I was needed on the phone.

"Grandpa passed away during the night," my mother tells me.

I'm shocked. It's not possible, we just got him out of the clutches of the other witch, he was fine, he seemed to be happy.

Seeing my defeated face, my manager understands that something serious has happened and authorizes me to leave. When I arrived at the nursing home, my parents were there; I threw myself into my mother's arms and cried. Only eighteen days, that's all! He lived for several years under the influence of Aunt-Nine and only enjoyed his newfound freedom for a short time.

Mom wants me to go into the room where my grandfather lies.

"You will see how beautiful he is. He is well dressed, I took care of him."

Dad doesn't agree with this idea. As for me, I am afraid that this image will disturb me and it is not the one I want to keep of my grandfather. Nevertheless, I enter the room. Beautiful? That's not the word I would use. He is no longer the same, he looks like a wax doll. I don't dare get too close, nor touch him.

Mom takes me to choose the casket. I don't listen to the salesman. I shrug my shoulders, I want to tell her that I don't want to choose, it's not up to me.

She brings Grandpa's body back home. She had the coffin placed in a room in the house and invited friends and family to pay their last respects to her father. I don't like this parade, I want to be alone. Why is Mom making this a festive event? She is excited that people are grieving for her, that they are interested in her - she likes that.

"Stop accepting that everyone comes to see grandpa dead! I don't like it, it's not a show!"

When I finally let go of what's on my mind, my parents don't understand me.

"You're really special!"

They deny that Mom is seeking attention through Grandpa's death.

On the day of the funeral, a religious ceremony takes place, decided by mom, although my grandfather was not at all religious. I put myself aside, I don't want anyone to hug me, to address me with this hypocritical kindness. I hold back my tears, I don't want to show my sadness, I don't want to be noticed. I watch Mom, she's crying, all the way in the front of the church, she turns around from time to time to make sure she's being watched.

Once the funeral is over, I prefer to go home, I don't want to go to my parents' house with all these people feeling sorry for us.

Invasive anxiety

In the summer of 2004, my mother's supervisor changed. At first, she seemed to like him, but as time went by, her inability to maintain good human relations became apparent, to the point that she ended up asking the doctor for a work stoppage, which she systematically renewed. Her income decreases as well as her morale. She does not try to understand the reason for her relationship difficulties, she prefers to blame everyone rather than question herself. She starts borrowing money again left and right. Besides, Paul is not very independent in his personal affairs, so he lets Mom manage his account. What a good deal!

Mom calls me at any time, crying, I have to come immediately. Since I don't live very far, I can't refuse. But every time, it's the same thing: I'm not the only one she called to be comforted. Always this desire to be noticed, without shame or modesty. I hate it, I hate seeing her like this, and that others see her like this. I am ashamed for her and I am not soft on her. She's slumped in her chair, crying, breathing hard, but it all sounds fake. What a good actress! She says she's going to kill herself, but I know she won't, I'm 21 and I've always heard her say that when things aren't going well. Her friends and colleagues are worried that she might actually go through with it. She claims that she is going to swallow a lot of medication, the ones she takes for her diabetes. I don't linger when I find her in this state, it exasperates me.

"I know your act, you won't do anything, I know it."

Each time it is an additional wound: no, she is not a real mother. So she will never change?

Paul looks sad to see Mom in this state. He seems to have compassion for her, which I don't understand. He, too, suffered her tantrums, her and his older brother's relentlessness in putting him down, humiliating him, making fun of him. He endured this torrent of nastiness that fell on him for no reason until he exploded, screamed, hit the walls, scarlet red, his eyes bubbling with tears. I felt sorry for him. I wanted to console him, to show him that I was on his side. But I preferred not to flinch, not to risk that their delirium targets me in turn. And then, I couldn't help but believe that everything we were accused of was logical. I couldn't question their words. Yes, we are idiots, our school results formally certify it: that's what they had managed to convince me of.

My mother is being sued by her employer, which is none other than the commune. She asks us to write certificates that she dictates to us. We all lie, once again, for her. She is trying to show that she is an honest, fair person, whom the elderly appreciate for her dedication. She tells us that the director and the "others at city hall" have turned their heads against her. At no time does she acknowledge what she is accused of.

It is such an upheaval that I don't feel well, but I can't express what I feel. I don't dare talk about all my anxiety with Damien, I am afraid he will think I am weird. My colleagues notice my discomfort and I end up confiding in one of them; but I don't understand what is happening to me, so how can I be helped?

It gets worse in September when, for the first time in the year and a half I've been working, I'm dealing with a deceased person. It's something I've always dreaded and been spared by my colleagues. But we are only two young employees and, what's more, two young employees who are not used to this situation. It is a difficult moment, the image of my grandfather is superimposed on that of the person we have to take care of. I come home late from work, I am anxious but I don't tell Damien. I isolate myself in the bedroom while he stays in the living room. I think about what could be causing my discomfort.

There is the difficult situation that mom is going through; I changed managers and at the same time sectors, so the colleagues are not all the same, nor the patients; moreover, as Damien and I are building our own house, we have moved in the meantime to the second home of one of his uncles. Did it all add up? I don't know, I can't manage my increasing anxiety on my own.

I will cling to Mom like a lifeline, as paradoxical as it may seem. The little girl she cared too much about resurfaces and seeks again from her what she has always sought but never found.

Mom gives me anxiolytics, she claims that they will relax me, help me sleep. I often go to see my doctor, I panic, I'm afraid. I'm afraid of having a disease, I'm afraid of dying. I am afraid of dying in my sleep, like when I was a child. He doesn't reassure me at all, he explains that I am a hypochondriac. He doesn't understand anything.

When my parents go on vacation, I feel abandoned. Who will I call at night when I panic all alone in my bed? Unconsciously, I let myself be absorbed by the past, I stick to mom like a magnet, I offer mom the possibility to attract me back to her possessive and poisonous love.

I call her even though she's far away, but she says there's nothing she can do to help me, that I should take one of those medications to relax, go to bed and that I'll be fine tomorrow.

I need someone to help me understand what is happening to me. I call Paul's girlfriend, I know she will find the right words to reassure me. She lives with her mother with whom I also get along well, she tells me to come and spend a moment with them. It's late, I tell Damien that I need to talk to them. I explain to them how I feel, that I feel like I have difficulty breathing, a pain in my chest, as if I were having a heart attack. I have digestive problems, heartburn. I hate to complain, but this is what I feel, and the more I feel this discomfort, the more I panic. They reassure me, they explain to me that it is the anxiety that causes these symptoms. However, they seem very real to me. I have pain everywhere, I feel that my muscles are contracted, I have pain in my shoulders, in my ribs... I can see that they do not understand what is happening to me. I feel like I'm going crazy. Damien also realizes that I am not well, that I am drifting. He must feel helpless in front of my distress, he doesn't understand anything either.

I decide to go see a physiotherapist, it will surely help me to relax.

During a consultation with my doctor, where my mother was present, they decided that I should see a psychiatrist. I agree, I am ready to do anything to find the origin of my malaise.

So I go to the consultation of a specialist who was advised to me by my general practitioner. I tell him about the anxieties which invade me, my fear of the disease, of death...

"Fear of dying is human, many people are afraid to die."

I understand that he doesn't see the need for this consultation, but I am not convinced by his arguments at all. I want someone who can find the origin of this malaise.

It is under these circumstances that the Christmas holidays are approaching. I'm dreading the Christmas Eve party at my parents' house with my youngest brother and his girlfriend. I ask Mom not to invite her older son: there's no way I'm eating at the same table as him. Mom sees how bad I feel about myself and doesn't know what to do to help me, so for once she doesn't push too hard and gives me the satisfaction. I don't know why, but the world oppresses me, I am afraid of dying during the meal, of collapsing in front of all the guests.

Mom has only one phone call to make and I come running: we both go shopping. I only have to choose, she buys me everything I want, dresses me from head to toe, pays my shopping cart...

I don't understand why she spends so much money on me and then a little while later she is devastated and asks for a loan? I refuse to comply with this request, it was not necessary to offer me again and again if she did not have the means. I am alternately the stupid kid or my mother's mother, depending on her needs.

It is in this emotional whirlwind and in this incessantly changing role-playing that the work on our house is about to be completed in early 2005.

I try to believe that after we move in, I'll get better. In the meantime, Damien and I decide to go on vacation, he's going to teach me to ski. I'm happy about this prospect, but I'm afraid to leave, why? I don't forget to bring my medication to calm my anxiety and those for my heart palpitations that sometimes get out of control.

The days in the mountains go well, but as soon as the evening arrives, I panic, convinced that I am going to die. Even though Damien is patient, I can see that I am annoying him. I am sure that only my mother can reassure me, but we are in the Pyrenees, far from the Charente-Maritime. I call her anyway. I would like to be able to calm myself, but it is too hard, I cannot. I'm curled up on the couch like the little girl I used to be, I'm shivering, I tell him my many symptoms over the phone, I tell him again how scared I am to disappear.

"You can't die without a reason, if you had a serious illness, you would have realized it a long time ago. You can't keep behaving like this, otherwise Damien will get fed up and he might leave."

His words comfort me, I can go to bed. Mom is right, I really have to shake it off, I have to stop putting myself in the shoes of a little girl who whines all day long, it's not bearable!

Damien blames me for not being able to live away from my mother, I know he is right, but I can't seem to get away from her; yet I want to.

We are considering a new evolution of our couple, especially me.

"What if we had a child?"

I think that the adventure of a pregnancy, the arrival of a baby that would be ours, could help my anxieties disappear.

We moved into our house in the spring. But I can't feel good about it, my psychological state is still not improving. I feel like a fussy child and that I wouldn't feel comfortable anywhere anyway.

"You have everything to be happy, there is no reason to have such ideas! Illness, death, you have to get it out of your head, damn it!

My chest hurts more and more often, it doesn't leave me, it feels like it's being squeezed in a vice.

One night, when it was at least 10 p.m., I was so panicked that I went to Dr. Pelletier's office. I know he's a late visitor. I hadn't seen him since my kidney problems and I was afraid he wouldn't want to see me with everything that had happened. But instead he welcomes me with a big smile. I tell him about all the pain I feel, my persistent uneasiness, my fear of dying. He examines me seriously, unlike the doctor I have been seeing lately, and does not take me for a hypochondriac.

"It's normal that you can feel all this with what you experienced as a child," he explains to me gently.

I am surprised that he dares to talk to me again about that time. I don't answer him or ask him any questions. I go back to bed, try to relax: I can believe it, I can't die like that, all of a sudden.

Dr. Pelletier has long since lost interest in my kidney problems. Mom passed the baton to me. I'm the only one running now.

In the hospital, it's no better, I'm there without being there. Sometimes, while I am lost in my thoughts, my eyes meet those of the elderly person I am supposed to take care of. I remain frozen, she seems to guess my distress, her eyes are so expressive that I feel compassion or pity, I am not sure. The panic prevails, I start to cry. I leave the room, I go to see one of my colleagues, Sophie, who, in my fantasies, replaces my mother. When I can't control myself anymore, I go to her and ask for an anxiolytic, the one my mother used to give me.

I blame myself for not being able to control my emotions in front of the patients, I have no right. They too would have good reason to be sad. They are at our mercy, their life ends here between the four walls of a hospital room in a geriatric ward, with the few photos left by the family. I want them to understand that I know how they feel in this place, with the staff as their only company; that I know the loneliness that eats away at them, there in their beds, when they are alone.

Sophie respects my silence about my discomfort. She does not ask me any questions. We meet together at a training session on "the end of life". I did not choose to participate, I was automatically enrolled, which does not help me to manage my anxieties.

A psychologist leads the training, which takes place over two days. I am anxious and confused. I hope that no one will notice, I know that if this happened, I would not be able to contain my emotions, which would put me in difficulty because of my inability to understand my condition and therefore to verbalize the reasons for it. It's as if I were the person at the end of life that the psychologist is talking about. But at lunch time, I broke down and told Sophie that I didn't want to go back, that I couldn't.

But I have no choice. I have to find a way to disconnect from the reality of what I'm hearing; I make my mind escape.

This ease for this shrink to relate the end of life, the death, shakes me. At the end of these two days, I have only one desire, to escape from here, I have to be the first one out. The shrink tries to hold me back and talk with me. I tell myself that I should give myself up to him without restraint, that he will perhaps find the deepest reason of my state. But no, I feel that he is going to ask me too many questions, I want to leave, no one can find what caused this internal tsunami.

A few weeks after this episode, my mother received an anonymous letter that seemed to be addressed to me and did nothing to ease my fears. The author describes the reasons why I had a kidney removed. He talks about manipulation, falsification of exams, children's judge, family separation

Mom is furious, she thinks that this letter was written by the wife of a doctor who took care of me when I was little and who is part of the town hall. According to her, she never appreciated it, and since my mother is always on trial because of her work, she would take advantage of it to add a layer.

My mother asked Dr. Brissaud for a letter contradicting these accusations so that she could present it to the courts. Despite my own annoyance at this anonymous letter, I find it quite amazing that Dr. Brissaud would agree to testify on my mother's behalf.

Knowing that someone has information about me, is leaking it, and is accusing my mother of having an organ removed makes me feel like my privacy has been violated. At the same time, I can't help but wonder: is it true that Mom had my kidney removed? It seems absurd to me, but, after all, she was kicking in and I know that exams were really falsified, I saw her do it with her son...

Madam,

I am writing to you regarding the problem of your daughter Delphine.

I would like to emphasize hereby that the removal of the left kidney that I had to perform on your daughter was not related to any forgery on your part and that the deterioration of her left kidney is in fact a sequel, on the one hand, of previous surgeries and, on the other hand, perhaps of a road accident that she had had, some time ago, and which could have completed a weakened left kidney and for which the vascularization was carried out in very bad conditions.

I am attaching the anatomical-pathological report of this left nephrectomy specimen which confirms that it was a diseased kidney and that the need for nephrectomy was obvious.

Doctor Brissaud, urologist, Nantes University Hospital.

Why is he taking her side? Hadn't something serious happened with those two angry doctors in Nantes? Could I ever find out?

A POSSESSIVE GRANDMOTHER

The test is positive! I run around the house, overjoyed, to tell Damien:

"I'm pregnant!"

This Saturday in July is the best day of my life. I can't wait to tell my mom the news too, I know she will be happy for me.

She is already telling me about all the things she wants to buy for the baby's arrival. I don't take her proposals seriously, I know that my parents are going through great financial difficulties. I let her tell my father the news, I don't dare tell him myself.

A month later, during my gynecological consultation, I reminded my specialist that I only have one kidney, while specifying that I did not want any particular follow-up. I want only the midwives to take care of me, that seems logical to me.

"Nevertheless, in case of problems, I am followed by Dr. Brunet.

- That's fine. But see him at least once in early pregnancy. I'll send him a letter."

Although this consultation does not seem useful to me, I accept. The nephrologist simply asks me to do a mid-pregnancy kidney ultrasound. This will be an opportunity to see my baby one more time, I thought.

On her side, mom doesn't mention this question of my kidney and the follow-up that it imposes in case of pregnancy.

Damien accompanied me to my first ultrasound in October. The radiologist, a specialist in obstetrical ultrasound, noticed that I only had one kidney.

"You are a carrier of a unique kidney.

- Yes," I said in a tiny, stealthy voice.

I'm afraid he'll ask me questions, but he doesn't add anything. I am relieved to see that he is only interested in the baby.

"The development of the fetus is going very well. I can already tell you the sex of the baby if you want."

We were moved and nodded.

"It's a girl."

I'm thinking of Mom: she'll be so happy to hear that!

She started to buy her lots of things, and we both spent whole afternoons shopping. She gives me baby equipment, clothes. I wonder if by accepting all this I am not allowing her to keep me dependent on her? She constantly talks about my baby even before my little girl is born, she invades her. I decide to stay vigilant, I don't want my mom to monopolize my little girl; I know that they would quickly become attached to each other, and that my daughter would risk putting me down to better value my mom. I am afraid that my mother will steal my daughter from me, but I also want my daughter to be independent, autonomous.

There is no way my mother will see my round, naked belly or even touch it. Her excitement about the upcoming arrival of this baby exasperates me. Of course, I don't dare to tell her, she'll get angry, pretend that I'm special and full of principles. Daddy will of course take her side.

I tell her that I want to take full advantage of my daughter, that I will breastfeed her. These moments, at least, will be mine alone, she won't be able to steal them from me.

I have thoughts that make me anxious. I am afraid of dying and not being there to protect and love my baby. If I die, Mom will be happy, she will be able to take my daughter, I won't be there to set limits. I want to talk to Damien about it, to warn him about what might happen if I disappeared, but he'd probably think I was crazy. I turn again to Paul's companion, who, when I tell her about my anxiety and fears, always finds the right words to reassure me.

I am living my pregnancy as a wonderful adventure, I am anxious to see my baby, but I am also apprehensive about my mother's behavior. How will I react if she is too eager to see my daughter? Won't Damien be left out if my mother takes up too much space? I feel alone and lost in the face of all her questions.

I have a little break in mid-January when my mother goes to take the nursing assistant exam in a neighboring department. Since she is known in our department for all the problems she caused her last employer, she had no other choice. She has to take the oral exam, she speaks well, I have no doubt that she will succeed. The jury in front of her doesn't know what kind of person she really is. As for me, she knows that I will not betray her. By my silence and my dependence, I have sacrificed myself for her survival.

She passed her exam, she is swimming in happiness, while I am missing everything I do and I don't feel happy despite my maternity leave and my soon to be full term pregnancy. Anger bubbles up inside me. I would like to take it out. But why, against whom?

What comforts me is that my mother may be far away the day my daughter is born, which is what worries her.

"I want to be there when my little 'babe' comes into the world."

His words disgust me, I want to be alone with Damien that day.

However, on the evening of March 14, it was as if I had forgotten all my fears. After a few moments of hesitation, I call my mother. She is on vacation, so she is at home. I tell her that we are leaving for the maternity ward.

Lila was born the next day at 5:30 pm. The midwives were giving her first aid when the phone rang in the delivery room.

"It's your mother who would like to come up and see you."

I can't believe it. It's been half an hour since my daughter was born, and she's already here, asking for it. She really has no restraint, the idea did not come to her to leave us a little intimacy, to wait for the next day? I am furious in spite of my exhaustion and refuse that she comes.

However, ten minutes after this call, she arrived. As only two people are allowed in the delivery room, Damien is asked to leave. I want to yell at her to get out of the way, to leave me with Damien. But instead of making my feelings clear to her, I shut down completely, don't talk to her, don't make any comments. She wouldn't listen to me anyway.

She is in awe of Lila who is in my arms. She is already boasting that she was the first to see her. She disgusts me.

As a midwife comes to accompany Lila and me to our room, Mom tries to hold the baby.

"Leave the baby on her mommy, please, she was just born, she needs to have her mommy's touch."

I thank this midwife inwardly, I would not have known how to say no to my mother, I think.

In fact, as soon as we are alone in the room, Mom rushes to ask for Lila. I don't answer, but I lift my hands that are on my baby to let her know that she can take her. I don't take my eyes off my little one, like a child who doesn't want to lend his toy. Except that a child would cry out, he would know how to show his displeasure, his anger. I remain a spectator, I can't express my emotions, my refusal to let myself be invaded by this too smothering mother. However, I am afraid that she takes my little princess into her diabolical web. She won't be able to defend herself either, I have to be there, always there, to fight against my mother's desire. But if I already can't refuse that she takes her in her arms a few hours after her birth, how will I manage to protect her later?

I need to show Mom that I am a good mother and that I don't need her. And by seeing me as such a wonderful mother, I want her to realize how bad she has been for my brothers and me.

However, after I returned home, Mom became more and more involved in my new family life. She comes to our house every day, she brings me each time a meal that she has cooked. She pretends that this prevents me from being too overwhelmed with the baby. She must think I am incapable of managing the new tasks that are imposed on the mother that I am.

Damien doesn't appreciate this daily intrusion but he doesn't say anything to her. It is on me that the reproaches fall:

"Can't you tell her to come less often? And she could knock before she comes in, this isn't a windmill here, you don't just walk in!"

I know he's right, I think the same as him, but I'm unable to answer him and, worse, unable to neutralize my mother's omnipresence. She'll get offended, humiliate me, I don't have the courage to face that.

"I'd rather spend my days with my cousin than see your mother at my house every day. It's not possible!"

I find it very hard to deal with this harshness and absence of Damien when he has taken his paternity leave to spend time with his baby. When I get up at night, I find that I am all alone with Lila. Damien comes home from his cousin's house quite late, probably as late as possible. I feed my daughter, crying. I don't think she can see my sadness.

The happiness I was waiting for for nine months is starting badly and it's because of my mother! Why because of her? Should we put some distance between us? Maybe I'm the one exaggerating the situation? Maybe I need her?

I'm confused.

I am home alone with my baby. I love her, but it's hard for me to realize that she's my daughter. I try to reassure myself, all young mothers must have the same feeling, right?

BUT WHY THIS UNEASINESS?

And so, despite the arrival of Lila and the life that is organized around her, two months later I still feel as lost as before my pregnancy.

At home, I feel like doing nothing, just devoting myself entirely to the baby. I take care of Lila after my work and her day at the nursery, Damien comes home, we eat, I put the little one to bed and go to my room to be alone. I curl up in bed and cry like a little girl. The worst part is that I still don't know why. The next day, I get up, the little girl leaves the place to the mom and faces this new day as well as possible for the well-being of Lila. I want her to be happy, to have good memories of her childhood, a "normal" life. But I'm completely neglecting Damien and even think that maybe it's because of him, because of our life as a couple, that I am like this. I find a lot of things to reproach him for and when I talk to my mother about it, she agrees with me. I'm ready to separate from him and move back in with my parents.

One Sunday, I share my wish with Damien. He doesn't understand, of course, since I haven't spoken to him for a long time, preferring my isolation to his presence. He cries, he does not want us to separate. Faced with his reaction, everything becomes confused: he loves me, I love him too, maybe we should just talk more.

At work, I surprise myself: I dare to have a certain critical spirit towards my colleagues and, timidly, I assert my ideas, whether I like them or not, I mention what bothers me in the establishment and propose solutions. But this new impetus makes me uncomfortable; my colleagues must not understand why little Delphine is "rebelling". I don't want to feel that I am not appreciated because I assert my ideas. I don't know how to behave anymore. Should I go along with it to keep pleasing my colleagues or should I "grow up" by continuing to assert myself?

I'm gradually detaching myself from the small group that mothered me from the moment I arrived in the department. I get to know other colleagues better. I sympathize a lot with one of them. I tell her about my uneasiness, my fears, my anxieties. She tries to help me by listening to me; for me, it is enormous to be listened to. She advised me to go and see a psychotherapist that she had already consulted. I am now ready to do anything to be helped, so that someone can finally tell me why I am so afraid of dying, a little more every day.

I go to my first appointment with the psychotherapist one afternoon in September, after work. I leave Lila at the nursery a little later than usual. I am both excited and tense. Excited because maybe I will finally discover the reasons for my unhappiness. Tense at the idea of the questions she will ask me, of what I will tell her.

I begin by describing to him the fears that invade me, the one of the disease that would lead to death, the pains that I feel, the death of my grandfather that affected me a lot, the problems of my mother with her work I cry without stopping, I would like to control myself, I find myself ridiculous, but I don't succeed.

The psychotherapist asks me questions about my pains, I am afraid that she thinks that they are imaginary, like my mother who kept telling me that I was causing them by obsessing about them, that they were psychological.

"There is indeed an event that torments you, the emotions you allow to appear demonstrate it."

Yes, but what's bothering me? If I came here, it's so that someone can help me find out.

The first session ends, we have made several appointments, I have to start a long term psychotherapeutic work. I don't believe in this necessity, it scares me. It seems to me that I have told her everything and that it is up to her to find the reason for my malaise.

On the second date, she tries to get some information out of me that could lead us to a lead.

"Didn't anything happen when you were a child? Our childhood experiences always follow us, and if we've repressed difficult things, they can come back to the surface as adults, for different reasons."

I understand and agree with this explanation. But I don't know what I might have repressed.

"No, no, it's been, there's been nothing special about my childhood. I was sick, but I'm better now."

No, it can't be my hospitalizations for my kidney that are tormenting me. It can't be. I am better now.

The session ends, I take the road to pick up Lila at the nursery. I don't feel like going back to see this psychotherapist, I'll have to call her to cancel the next appointments. There is also the question of the financial aspect: I cannot afford the fee, which is not reimbursed. For these first two sessions, it was mom who paid.

A few days later, I decide to talk with my mother about the issue raised by the shrink.

"You can't believe everything the shrinks say. I don't understand why you get so worked up. You have everything you need to be happy: Damien, a nice house, a beautiful little girl.

I feel like I'm not moving forward, no one can help me, I'm struggling to find the reason for my discomfort, all my efforts are going nowhere and my condition is getting worse.

I feel like everything is going wrong, I would like to change jobs, the pace doesn't suit me anymore, I am completely out of step.

But why this uneasiness?

I don't want to be a caregiver anymore, I don't want to wear this uniform. I have a very hard time with my daughter, I want to take care of her alone, to be autonomous, not to need someone to take her to or pick her up from the daycare. On the weekends when I'm not the one taking care of her, my mother does it. She keeps her at home, but it is still her who spends the day with my daughter, not me. It's getting harder and harder to take.

A first tear will take place at Easter, when we are invited to lunch at my parents' house. My mother warns me that morning that her oldest son will be there. She doesn't want me to make a fuss, she knows that I refuse to come to a family meal in her presence.

"Make an effort to please me, I'll be happy to have my three children together."

She takes the opportunity to tell me about our vacation from which we returned a month earlier with Damien and Lila. She tells me that her oldest son is constantly criticizing our stay in the mountains. Is she telling me this now on purpose to test my ability to control myself in front of this guy I can't see? So many questions, with no answer of course.

During the meal, I find myself sitting right in front of him. I hate his look, it still bothers me as much as in my childhood. He starts, he attacks, he addresses multiple reproaches to me then comes to evoke our vacations in the snow I react to the quarter turn. I retort by insulting him. I hate being rude, but with him, I can't do otherwise, it's my only means of defense. The more I insult him, the more he gets angry. He gets up, hits me violently on the head with his hand, leaves the room like a fury, takes his bike and leaves.

"As usual, you're ruining the family meal!" my father tells me.

"I'm warning you, if anything happens to her, it's your fault!" my mother says.

If she knew how much I care! Paul starts to insult me in his turn, it's the first time he's attacked me with such virulence. His girlfriend says nothing, embarrassed.

Neither my brother nor I want to see each other again. As for Damien, I am disgusted, he could have defended me. He said nothing, did nothing.

No one cares if I was hurt, if I'm okay. We go home, we don't talk. Even Damien is mad at me! I take an aspirin, that slap gave me a headache. We continue to go about our business without talking about this event again.

A CONFUSING RELATIONSHIP

In September 2007, I decided to resume my studies. I went back to university to prepare a diploma of access to university studies (DAEU) in literature (equivalent to the baccalaureate) paid for by my employer. I study French, history, geography and English. I appreciate this distance from my work.

While I was in training, the nursery called me one day to tell me that Lila had a temperature. I advised them to give her some Doliprane and called my mother to ask her to go get her.

"I think she'll be better off in the quiet, I'll be there as soon as I get out of class," I tell her.

I'm on my way when my mother calls me back to tell me she's taking Lila to her primary care physician. Angrily, I hang up the phone and speed up. My mother has no business taking my daughter to a doctor! A doctor that Lila doesn't know, and she's being treated by a pediatrician. What does my mother care about, how dare she take this right? I don't take my daughter to the doctor for the slightest fever! At this age, it could be her teeth, her growth, nothing to panic about right away!

When I arrive, they are still in the waiting room. This doctor doesn't know Mom very well, nor does he know much about the problems I've had. He examined Lila and lectured me:

"You know, a child can have a fever for no obvious reason. Just give them paracetamol and only come in if the temperature persists after forty-eight hours."

I am beside myself and I think he realizes it. I'm so mad at my mom for making me look like an angsty person who takes her daughter to the doctor all the time.

No more asking my mom to pick up Lila when she has a fever. I don't care if I have to leave my class to take care of my daughter.

After nine months of training, I did not obtain my DAEU. I was disappointed, but not surprised.

My life is back to normal: work, daycare. Now, Mom is watching Lila when Damien and I both work on weekends, but I don't want to let her sleep over. The hours she spends at my parents' house leave me anxious enough.

One day, I came home without knocking to pick up the little one after work. I find Lila lying on the couch, carefully wrapped in a blanket. My heart racing, my blood boiling, I remove the blanket, take my baby in my arms.

"She's not well, she has a fever, she's resting."

I don't dare say anything, but I don't think less of my daughter's alleged fever. As soon as she gets home, she plays with her toys.

On several occasions, I have also found Lila sitting on my mom's lap in front of the TV, watching a DVD that Grandma bought her. I don't like the fact that she won't let my daughter play alone and makes her watch the screen. I'm worried. Mom is weaving her poisonous web around Lila. Lila will gradually become mentally paralyzed if I don't do something. I feel like I'm going to lose my daughter.

During this confusing relationship period between my mother, Lila and me, I learned that I was pregnant. This pregnancy was expected, but Damien and I decided not to tell my mother at this time. On several occasions, we heard her proclaim that she only loved Lila, that she could never love another child.

"It's only Lila that matters to me."

I decided to break with what made me dependent on my mother and to impose limits between her life and mine. I no longer give her my laundry to iron, I refuse to let her do the shopping together. But how can I justify myself? How will she take it? Will she reject me? Imposing my choice, which did not suit Mom, made me feel abandoned.

My relationship with my mother is becoming more and more conflicted. We regularly fall out, but each time, she calls me right after so that we can make up. I can't take it anymore, she wears me down, I'm tired.

"You're going to kill me, I can't take it anymore!" I sometimes say to her before hanging up.

Damien realizes the difficulties I have with my mother, that this relationship is becoming difficult for me. But he gets angry when I explain that I am afraid to tell my mother how I feel.

It's okay if I hurt Mom's feelings, it's okay if I shatter her illusions of a close relationship between us; in fact, I want to shatter all those illusions that are false... I need to maintain a healthy balance with my family, Damien, Lila, our unborn baby and me.

So I make the decision to tell Mom about some changes. I feel ready to face whatever it takes to gain my freedom and protection for my daughter.

"You won't have to take Lila to the nursery in the morning anymore, I'm changing my hours, I'll only do 1:30-9:30 from now on. And on weekends, we'll make arrangements with Damien so that one of us is always home.

- What are you blaming me for? You won't be able to stand working every afternoon anyway. You'll soon come to me for help again, you'll see!"

Wickedness shines in his eyes.

"She's my ray of sunshine, Lila, what will become of me without her?"

She makes me mad. This is what she would like to get into Lila's head: Grandma can't live without you.

"We'll come to see you and Lila once a week, depending on my day off. I'll come after her nap, and we'll stay until evening."

I am imposing the rules now.

And I can't help but think more and more that the psychotherapist was right: maybe my experience as a little girl, my hospital past, are at the origin of this internal confusion. I try to solicit my mother. I ask her to meet a psychologist together, so that she can help me remember; she agrees, but does not make the appointment. I suggest that we go and see Dr. Brissaud: he will tell me what happened, the truth about the whole story. Once again, she agrees, but does not make the appointment. However, it was always her who made the appointments.

She is only concerned about Lila:

"Why are you depriving me of my granddaughter? I need her so much, plus right now I'm not in the mood."

This is an argument that reinforces my choice. Lila is certainly not a toy or a little pet. Lila is a child who must live her life to the fullest as a little girl; a life full of carefree fun that leaves no room for adult problems.

As for me, I don't intend to let go of my mother. If she doesn't want to meet with specialists, I at least want her to answer my questions.

"Mom why did you tap my kidney when I was little, why did you falsify the lab results, what was that about the juvenile judge?

- What the hell is wrong with you? Why are you talking to me about this again?

- Do you remember the psychotherapist I saw? I think that maybe she was right, maybe my childhood experiences are at the root of my malaise.

- Nonsense, you and your shrinks! You shouldn't believe everything they tell you. And if I did all that, it was for your own good, so that the doctors would understand that you were really sick."

She starts to cry, I start to cry. We have to calm down quickly, my father will come home, Lila will wake up.

But I decide not to leave it at that. "It was for your own good"? This puzzles me. If the doctors didn't think I was sick, why would she want to show them that there was something wrong with me? I need to know for sure and I want Dad to be there this time. Maybe he'll stand up for me, he might not agree with what my mom said.

"What the hell are you trying to do to us fifteen years later with this? If your mother did that, it was for your own good. You're pissing us off with all your questions!!!"

I made daddy angry, he leaves and slams the door.

I don't know what to think. I take more and more distance with mom. I understand that my confusion comes from her, from the relationship we have, from her possessiveness. I have to detach myself from this pressure that Mom puts on me.

Mom realizes that I want our relationship to evolve, but not in the way she would like. She regularly asks me why she can see Lila less. I give various reasons: I don't have time... it's better this way...

"There is a law that gives rights to grandparents. If I go to court, I'll see her more, the judge will impose visitation and custody times for us. You won't have a choice."

I am revolted. How could the justice give him this right after his behavior with me? I don't know everything, but I know that it must have been serious. The anger of the doctors, the judge of the children, the falsification of the analyses, the punches on the kidney... It is only me, her and her elder son who know it, but to make mom understand that she must change, that our relationship must change, I am ready to reveal our secret, to seek the truth. I am ready to betray mom, I don't care about the consequences for her.

More than a year after I broke up with my youngest brother, I met his girlfriend by chance. I had always gotten along well with her, and for some time I had been wanting to reconnect with Paul. I started talking to him about everything that was bothering me about my hospitalizations, my kidney, my mom's behavior with Lila...

Some time later, I take advantage of the birth of their baby to approach them. We visit them in the maternity ward. My sister-in-law noticed that Mom was not behaving very "normally". I feel understood and tell her about my second pregnancy. Except for Damien, no one knew about it until then.

I now decide to confide in Damien, who only knew about a kidney operation I had undergone when I was a child. I don't know what he thinks of my story. I cry, he remains silent.

One weekend, while I was at work, Mom took advantage of my absence to call Damien and invite us to eat at her house. She knows that Damien, even if he doesn't feel like it, will accept to please her. I think Mom thinks that my current behavior is a spoiled child's whim and that she can get Damien to help her change my mind. I have to admit that I'm afraid she's not going to succeed. Even though Damien knows a little bit about my history, he may not have believed me and may be lulled to sleep by Mom's nice speech.

So on July 12, 2008, she brings us together, Paul, his partner, their little boy, Damien, Lila and me. I suspect that something will happen, that this meal is a way for her to get what she wants.

I put Lila in her pajamas in one of the rooms, Mom joins me and takes advantage of the fact that we are alone to ask me to leave Lila with her one afternoon to take her on the merry-go-round.

"No, there's no way, if you want to see her ride, you'll come and watch her, but Damien and I will be the ones taking her, we want to enjoy our weekend with our daughter."

I join Damien to tell him my brief discussion with mom and to share with him my state of irritation.

"We won't stay long, we'll pretend that Lila is tired and escape from here," I said.

In the middle of the meal, my mother approached Damien and asked if she could take Lila on a ride. I can't believe her nerve! I rush to answer and refuse.

"I will sue you, grandparents have rights!"

I look her straight in the eye:

"If you do that, I'll ask the juvenile judge to reopen my case, I'll research my hospital history, I'll get the whole story out, and it'll be you that the situation turns against!"

I gather our things to leave. I want this fight to start a burst of all Mom's secrets, all her unhealthy manipulations.

"Go ahead, Paul, tell her that you know about the 30,000 euros she stole from you during all these years, about the transfers from your account to hers that she made without your knowledge! We had to go through your bank statements one by one to find out!

Mom sits in a chair crying.

"I just have to shoot myself in the head, if you think I'm that bad."

Dad left, slamming the door, I think he doesn't understand what's going on, he never tried to understand, his passivity in front of the events of our family opened the way to the power and the authoritarianism of mom, to the hold she has on us.

Her words don't touch me, she won't change my mind.

"It would be better if we took some real distance."

She follows us to the car and asks me if she can still see Lila. I lie to her:

"But no, I'll never stop you from seeing Lila, only, we'll stop seeing each other for a while, it will do us good."

I know in my heart that it was the right thing to do. I have no desire to go back, I will not go back to her. No she won't see Lila again, no she will never change. This breakup is going to allow me to get out of this evil hold that Mom has on me, on Lila.

All these years of silence, of loneliness, have allowed me to recognize the taste of the undetectable poison for others! Thanks to this rupture, I will be able to start a hard work, that of looking for all my medical files, to see again all the doctors who took care of me at the time. I want to retrace my entire history. This is to perhaps succeed in stabilizing myself, in understanding the inner turmoil that has haunted me all this time. I can only do this by being separated from her.

A confusing relationship

I have spent the last two years struggling with my mother's possessiveness towards Lila and I realized that I needed to stop this possessive relationship between mom and me first.

Putting the pieces together

The first doctor I saw was Dr. Hacquin. I told him right away that I had no health problems, that I only wanted to talk to him about what had happened when I was "sick". He agrees to tell me my story. Damien is present.

"Your mother did everything she needed to do to appear to be a good, caring, devoted mother. In medical terms, it's called Munchausen's syndrome by proxy. She was falsifying test results, the doctors also had doubts about the ECBU's, they wondered if she was adding something before bringing them to the lab. A report was made to the children's judge, and the doctors recommended removing the child from the family and placing her in care. This solution was not retained, you seemed too disturbed to be separated from your mother."

Before leaving, he takes me in his arms.

"You're doing great, you've become a good person."

His words give me confidence and make me want to continue, to move forward.

I am stunned: he confirmed most of my memories. On the other hand, it is the first time I hear about Munchausen's syndrome by proxy. While searching on the Internet, I find all kinds of sites that evoke this syndrome and I find indeed common points with mom's behavior.

I must continue my research, I want to know, I want to know everything and meet all the doctors who had a role in this completely hallucinating story.

The first form I got to retrieve one of my medical records was from Professor Verneuil in Bordeaux, which I remember. I answered his secretary's questions, she verified that my file was properly archived. My heart is pounding at the thought that I will soon be holding official documents of my history in my hands.

Two days after our breakup, Mom comes back to me. She calls me several times a day, I never pick up, I want her to understand that my decision is firm and final. She comes to the house, tries to open the door, which is locked.

One evening, while we are at my brother's house for his friend's birthday, our mother, who was not invited, bursts into his house, crying. She wants him to come out, she wants to talk to him. My brother refuses. She leaves like a fury, shouting that she is going to crash, that she wants to put an end to her life. This rather violent intrusion cools the atmosphere. I am not surprised, she likes to make a spectacle of herself. She even forgot her cell phone. Voluntarily, I think. My brother receives a call from a friend of Mom's at whose house she has gone whining.

A few weeks later, we received a summons from my parents' lawyer. They asked for visitation and accommodation rights for Lila. I can't believe they did it! I decided not to respond, to wait and see what would happen. After all, it wouldn't hurt to have it decided by a court. With our past, she can't get what she wants. The letter specifies that we have fifteen days from the receipt of the summons to instruct a lawyer to act for us, failing which a judgment may be rendered on the arguments provided by the plaintiffs alone.

I think Mom wants to show me that she's still in charge. She thinks she can devastate everything in her path, forget about it and go on her way as if nothing had ever happened. I've been forgetting for twenty-five years now, repressing my emotions and feelings. It's time to relive them to access my true inner self!

In support of the lawyer's letter, there are testimonials from people who are saddened, who feel sorry for her or whatever. There are also photos showing Lila at my parents' house. With her little chicken, with her grandmother, her grandfather. In anger, I tear up the pictures.

I have already removed all the pictures where my mother appears. I won't forget her face, nor her fake expression, but I don't want anything that reminds me of her physically, I don't want to see her anymore!

September 1st, 2008

Since July 15, 2008 we have not heard from you, don't you think it would be nice if you came home and we could talk, because it would be a shame for the family to be torn apart like this, for reasons we don't understand.

There is still time for you to back out before it is too late.

We would like to see Lila, not to erase these two and a half years where she brought us a lot of happiness and would like to see her grow up like all grandparents. We think, me and your father, don't deserve what you have been doing to us for the last month and a half.

The door is always open to you and we would love to have you back.

Mom.

To both of you,

Don't think that mom is manipulating me to write, as you already told me Delphine: I take my responsibilities.

Not seeing Lila anymore makes us very unhappy.

Putting the pieces together

To break up a family life suddenly is hard for us to bear. It is imperative that you come back home or that you give us some news. To be forced to obtain a court decision to assert our rights is surely not the best solution.

So, I beg you, there is always time to go back and then only fools don't change their minds.

Life is still long!

Dad.

Come back, certainly not! Did I deserve everything I went through because of her? She is convinced that everything she put me through was not to harm me, she has no idea how I felt during all those years of hospitalization, all those years when she made me dependent on her, when she injected me with her venom that took away my life impulse.

I finally have almost all the missing pieces of the puzzle about the truth of this story.

My body, all those doctors stole it from me, cut it up, searched it, mutilated it. I felt so often humiliated, all for nothing! All of them were content to carry out the examinations to look for the origin of these pains alleged by mom and me, without asking themselves any question!

It was my sacrifice against his love.

Now she would like me to forget about it and continue to have a good relationship with her, not to tear the damn family apart brutally!

The doctors sometimes wondered, but Mom's relentless determination left no doubt.

Everything is racing through my mind, I feel a lot of guilt: why didn't I tell the doctors the truth? Why didn't I do anything to help myself? I start to cry. I have to tell them the truth today.

I have to tell her too that I know what she did. I feel the anger in me. Anger at her but also at me. I regret having agreed to "play" with her!

I want her to have regrets, I want to hear her cry for me!

Reclaiming a stolen childhood

In September 2008, I had an appointment with Professor Brissaud, whom I had not seen since June 2000.

"Your mother is a total nut job, get the hell away, she'll never leave you alone."

I think I remember, but I am afraid to remember. He tells me about Mom's constant phone calls, always very alarming about my condition, about the falsified analyses, especially one, the one that alerted him. He takes responsibility for the loss of my kidney.

"I injected an anesthetic into your kidney tissue to relieve your pain. It was this injection into a kidney weakened by previous procedures and a car accident that caused your kidney to become non-functional. It was my fault, not your mother's. When I became aware of the falsification of an analysis, I asked colleagues for their opinion, which led me to refer the matter to the juvenile judge."

No, I don't agree, it's not his fault that he had to remove my kidney. I want to tell him, on the contrary, that he is my saviour, that it is thanks to him that everything has stopped. But the words get stuck in my throat.

I told him about my time at the Bordeaux University Hospital, in the department of Dr. Verneuil. But he did not understand, he had never heard of this doctor.

He tells me that I should request a copy of my file, the one he has in front of him. He tells me where to go to request it. I feel like I still have a lot to understand. I hope my file will help me.

When I went to pick up Lila from daycare a few days later, I learned that my mother had come. She had entered the premises without warning and asked to see her granddaughter. I was forced to explain my relationship with my mother and my current approach, which I had previously avoided.

My mother's relentlessness scares me a little. She'll do anything to see Lila, despite the procedure she's initiated. When she tries to come to the house, I close the electric blinds so she can't see me through the window, call Damien, even though he can't do anything from where he is, and notify the police, even though they refuse to intervene in a family dispute.

A family dispute resulting from abuse and for which a procedure is underway!

When I received my file from the Nantes University Hospital, I was shocked. My memories combined with all this paperwork show me how serious the whole process for these damn kidney problems is.

Yet, I still find it hard to believe. I keep telling myself that it was okay, that it wasn't so bad. What could be more normal for a child than to sacrifice herself for her mother? "And then, it was mom who knew, she was certainly exaggerating, but I was probably a little sick." This is the idea she managed to instill in me, her words that became mine and that even today, soak my brain. How can shrinks help me, if I can't even get rid of this web that Mom wove?

Yet I want to succeed. I know I can do it. I have managed to decipher the bond that keeps me attached to her: my quest for the deepest relationship there is, the relationship to mother. Any relationship that brings me the intensity of the one I have with Mom scares me. I keep myself apart, I protect myself, I defend myself. I have never been able to assert myself, to rebel frankly. Today, I want to be able to do so and I am gradually gaining confidence in myself. Little by little, I perceive that I am a person quite distinct from my mother.

I asked the midwife, during my monthly follow-up for the pregnancy of my second child, to be able to take a leave of absence from work; I feel physically fit to continue my work but not psychologically. I mention some important personal worries that I don't feel able to manage in addition to my work and my family life. In truth, I want to devote myself to the search for my past history. I will now race against time. I want to have this story unraveled, I want to try to rebuild and stabilize myself before my baby arrives.

I decided to call the mother and child hospital of the CHU of Nantes to try to speak with Dr. Gauthier. I was told that he had recently retired. So I contacted the telephone information service. They gave me two names that could correspond to the doctor in Nantes. I dialed the first number: answering machine; it did not seem to be him. I dial the second number. I have a lump in my stomach. How will I introduce myself? Will he remember me? Maybe he will think that my approach is not important?

"Hello?

- Hello, you saw me when I was a child.

- Yes, for what reason?

- You have made the diagnosis of Munchausen's syndrome by proxy.

- You are little Delphine, next to La Rochelle."

I sit down. I can't believe it, he remembers me. He agrees that we should talk about my story. He suggests an appointment at the hospital where he goes once a week.

I now decide to get the contact information of Dr. Carrez, who has also left the hospital. He too remembers me. I will meet him much later.

Things are progressing, little by little, I am gathering all the elements that allow me to reconstitute my history, I am in the process of reappropriating it.

When I met Dr. Gauthier, he began by telling me that he thought I was fine. He thought he would find a more disturbed woman. I don't know how I should take it. I don't know how I should take it, especially since even though I don't look disturbed, I'm in total chaos inside. He has my file on the desk, he shows me the analysis that was falsified by mom, the one that allowed the doctors to make a report to the judge of the children. I don't learn much more than with Dr. Hacquin or Dr. Brissaud. But I can put a face on this angry doctor who made a strong impression on me at the time. In this process, it is important that I can picture the people. And it makes me feel good that the doctors are talking to me and not to Mom, to realize that they don't see me as her accomplice. I can finally try to express what the little girl was feeling, even if it is still difficult.

My file also contains documentation on Münchhausen syndrome by proxy, which dates from that time. So they took this case seriously, so they could help me. At the time, I only thought they were trying to separate Mom and me.

"I have encountered very few cases like yours. Once, a mother arrived with her child, who had fainted and lost consciousness. The mom had skillfully induced this fainting with an insulin injection."

So I am a rare case, but my mother is not the only one who seeks the admiration of the medical profession. These women are really sick.

"You should still let your mother continue to have a relationship with your daughter, in a neutral, supervised place. You don't need to be vengeful."

Of course I don't want to be vengeful, but I fear that this relationship between Lila and my mother would not allow me to mark this break between me and my mother. Lila would remain between Mom and me as the cause of an ongoing conflict in which she would find herself embroiled and which would perhaps make our own mother-child relationship complicated.

Dr. Carrez told me, during our telephone conversation, not to go back.

As at the time, Dr. Carrez clearly leaned towards a very prolonged separation while Dr. Gauthier thought that a strict medical follow-up could still be tried. In any case, they both note that my evolution, in spite of my rather complex past, is rather positive and notice that the man with whom I share my life accompanies me in my approach and tries to understand with me.

A few days later, I received a call from a psychologist at the Bordeaux University Hospital. She warned me that the report of her consultation could not be part of the copy of my file that I had requested, because it was not a medical document. I have no memory of this psychologist. I explain to her the reasons for my request and what I have been through. She told me that at the time she had recommended a family separation because of a complicated mother-daughter relationship. Already when I was 6 years old they wanted to separate us! It's strange that I don't remember that.

I have many questions about this selective memory.

Mom had never told me about this interview with this psychologist. But I understand better why we never came back to this hospital.

I also find it amazing that my mother did not tell Dr. Brissaud about my previous hospitalizations when she brought me to Nantes. I am convinced that if he had known the exact content of the La Rochelle file and the Bordeaux file, he would have certainly alerted Dr. Gauthier and Dr. Carrez much earlier. I might still have my kidney right now.

I am caught up in all these discoveries, and time flies; it is November 2008, and I have not worked for about two months already. I spend my days and nights putting together the scattered pieces of my story. I am also very worried about the procedure my mother has started, I am afraid she will get what she wants. Only I can detect and understand my mother's mechanism. How could the judges realize her manipulations and have the heart to deprive grandparents of their grandchildren? Every day, as I go through my files, I move heaven and earth to make my right to distance myself from my family heard. I don't know where I find all my energy and moral strength. But I have the impression that I will succeed, with the agreement of justice or not! Today, I am the one who makes the decisions. I am no longer the submissive little girl that my mother made me.

My mother understands that we are no longer a unit and that I am ready to do anything to protect my daughter. She continues to keep an eye on me, coming to the nursery at any time to see Lila, phoning my mother-in-law to get useful information for her procedure.

To stop her in her tracks, I decide to go to the gendarmerie. An officer takes my statement for a preliminary investigation. I describe my experience, my relationship with my mother, my fears for my daughter, the reasons for my approach and the procedure in progress. I give them the medical files I have. He makes photocopies that he attaches to the hearing. I ask that an officer goes to my parents' home to explain to my mother that she must stop bothering me in my daily life, that she must wait for the court decision. The gendarmes are listening, they don't judge. It may not be much, but for me, it is a lot.

November 24, 2008
Delphine and Damien,

I take the pen again so I can talk to you. Mom knows about it, of course. I alone made this decision. Once again I beg you, on behalf of Lila and for her sake, to reconsider your decision to stop showing her to us and to prevent us from being able to kiss her.

On Christmas Eve, it is unbearable to see her suppress the joy of bringing her stocking under the tree and discovering a gift the next day, like the last two years. It's like when you, Delphine, brought the chicks for Lila and she plays with them. You saw, she loves them. So why? Delphine, you think I'm fine, but you're wrong. I'm hiding a lot of things.

Children should not be deprived of the joy they feel especially at Christmas time.

I am aware that you may have grievances with us. Mistakes may have been made, but under no circumstances should the children pay the price. For two and a half years you trusted us when you needed us, and we were always there. We had everything in duplicate to make things easier.

Your daughter Lila at that time was never exposed to any danger.

I still believe that we need to talk and put things straight. It is through dialogue that we can find a solution. Of course, you have to want it strongly. As you know, a procedure has been started, but one gesture on your part and it stops.

We count on your kindness and sensitivity as parents to analyze this letter with indulgence, obviously thinking of the interest of the children. We know that you are expecting a new child and it would be a pity if he/she could not know his/her grandparents. The problems of grown-ups should not disturb the world of children where only love and happiness have room. You are certainly disturbed, but we are very unhappy about this situation.

The idea of not being able to provide and live the role of grandparents is a great frustration.

Meditate on these words, know that it is never too late. The door to the house is always open. A word, a gesture, a reflection, a resignation will always be a good solution.

Dad.

Reading this letter makes me smile gently. My father really doesn't understand anything. My mother has brainwashed him; he is beyond repair, unfortunately.

I think that, like all children, I loved my parents without them needing to command me. Today I realize that this love was exploited and I was abused. I can now allow myself to think that my mother, whatever her reasons, did not love me since she made me a victim without caring about my feelings, my psychic pain or my future... This awareness helps me to free myself from the feelings of guilt that have been destroying me. By referring her actions to my mother, I free myself.

To go further in my approach I go to see a hypnotherapist. As we came to speak about sophrology, I explained to her that this process was not unknown to me. I describe to her physically the man who came to the house, I even remember from which city he came.

"It's amazing that a sophrologist consults at home".

She doubts. Nevertheless, she thinks she knows him, she would have done her sophrology studies with him. She gives me his name and advises me to contact him, he could teach me something about my history.

After this first session, I already know that I will not come back. I think that this way of operating will not suit me. In my opinion, positive thinking is not a remedy at all, because it is a form of self-mystification, it is an escape from reality, which cannot be a help, because the body knows what it is. All these muscle pains, palpitations, headaches... If I couldn't feel how the little girl suffered in the past, my body would let me know and I could trigger an illness. I am convinced that our psychology affects the body.

I know I will have to find someone to help me. I don't want to condemn myself. I know that I am capable of knowing the truth about what it was like to be a little girl.

In my quest for the truth, I went to see the child psychiatrist I had met during the whole judicial upheaval that almost led to the family separation. I didn't remember him, but I found his name in the letters in my files.

"How was I, how did my mother behave? Why did my father let her?

- Your father seemed to agree with your mother. He didn't realize the seriousness of his actions."

He is one of the few people who have met him and therefore can support the idea that my mother also completely manipulated my father.

He gives me copies of the letters in my file and advises me to be accompanied. He gave me the names of two psychiatrists.

I go to one of them. But I feel like he is making excuses for my mother. I can't agree to keep giving myself up if he thinks I don't have the right to hate her. When I leave his office, I feel like I don't understand anything. I need time, to be alone, to study, to reread, to file, to strive to remember. It is as if the adult I am today needs to relive the life of the little girl.

I think I need to give myself the time and patience to fully emerge from this long emotional sleep. It was in the terror of hospitalizations, the consultations with all those doctors, the conversations of worried adults about me, in this insecurity that my childhood took root. In the impossibility of expressing my true feelings for fear of disappointing my mother, of making her more ill than she already was. Expressing my true feelings at that time would have turned our lives upside down and we would have been very unhappy.

I get the files from Dr. Brunet, the nephrologist in La Rochelle, and from the surgery department, directly on the spot because I am followed in this hospital for my pregnancy. I leaf through them in the waiting room. In the first one, I discovered letters addressed to various doctors of which I have no trace in my other files and which I do not remember having consulted. Was Dr. Brissaud aware of this? In the second one, I am dismayed to read that I had no "anomaly". However, I will be operated on, the first operation on my kidney. What happened?

I go to see the secretary, I want to see the surgeon who operated on me. Since he no longer practices here, I ask for Dr. Lemoine who examined me at the request of the nephrologist. Maybe he will explain to me why I had all these operations when my tests were normal. I feel anger rising inside me.

The surgeon is in his office, he agrees to meet me. I cry, the letters I have just read make the elements of my story even more incomprehensible.

"Why did the doctors let my mother take me for a consultation, why did no one stop her in this hellish race when the tests showed that I was fine? Why did they end up operating on me, why so many doctors, so many hospitals in so little time? Is a child not protected when the mother brings the diagnosis already prepared to the doctors? We are not safe when we are children!

- I understand your distress, miss, but I can't help it, I'm not the one who operated on you."

I left that office devastated. This doctor had tried to help me at the time by writing that I needed psychological follow-up, but he didn't go any further in his questioning about the complaints about my health that my mother was telling. And today, he can't answer anything else.

I decided to contact the nephrologist in La Rochelle. But unfortunately, he continued to agree with my mother. He dares to tell me that it is the fault of the hospital in Nantes if I lost my kidney. According to him, the injection of Marcaine carried out by Doctor Brissaud is responsible. But Dr. Brissaud simply did not know what to do to stop the pain that my mother and I were talking about.

Even as I discover the extent of my mother's insanity, she consults a psychiatrist to prove that she is "fit" to care for her granddaughter.

I, the undersigned doctor Purgon certify that I met today Mrs. Robin Martine.

During this interview, I did not note any signs of psychological suffering or behavioral problems that would be of concern to her or to others.

Certificate prepared at the request of the person concerned and delivered by hand.

Having only mom's version, and apparently seeing her for the first and last time, he has no opportunity to give any opinion. I don't find him very professional. I hope that the justice will mandate an expert psychiatrist, who will be able to hear all the people concerned.

But the more the months go by, the more worried I am. The evidence presented by my parents' lawyer seems strong. I find it hard to understand how my mother can be defended. Her lawyer knows absolutely nothing about the truth of our history or the reasons behind my breakup with my family. But Mom can be ruthless in getting what she wants.

So I think more and more that we should be seen by a psychiatrist. I could explain to him my fears, my background; he could, I think, have an objective and fair opinion on the issue of grandparents' rights.

I phone Dr. Carrez, he can give me some advice. He sent me a letter in February 2009, which he advised me to send to the judge.

I hereby confirm the general terms of our recent brief telephone communication, as agreed:

- It is not possible for me to offer any authoritative viewpoint on your particular current situation.

- On the other hand, it is a very good thing, it seems to me, that the questions which arise for you (access to grandparents) are presented in terms of psychiatric expertise. It is indeed highly desirable that all the persons concerned be able to undergo a very precise psychological evaluation in view of the risks which have already been incurred by yourself and which are present in the Munchausen syndrome by proxy.

- I am repeating generalities: if I cannot pronounce on your particular situation, I can confirm that it is absolutely necessary, in such circumstances, that the persons who will be led to formulate opinions should be able to do so, from both the legal and medical points of view, by surrounding themselves with information, and

Victor was born on February 15, 2009. I entrusted Lila to the person in charge of the nursery; I did not want Damien's mother to take care of her, I know very well that my mother would have known that we had left for the maternity hospital and would have immediately gone to my mother-in-law's house to see her. I can imagine her crying, telling my daughter that I'm mean, that it's because of me that they are separated. I already feel like I'm in trouble as a mom. I think I'm doing the transfer in spite of myself. Lila: the little girl I was. Me, the adult of today: my mother of yesteryear. I know it will work out in the end, one day I will find the time and the person, and the journey will happen.

I asked the staff of the maternity hospital that my stay be confidential, I fear that my mother will take advantage of this moment of joy to come and try to renew the links. Indeed, the day after Victor was born, my mother called the hospital to see if I was there. But confidentiality means anonymous, and this time I don't feel the need to hold my baby all the time. I happily let him sleep in his own bed. I think about myself, I take care of myself, I get dressed, I put on makeup. With him, I immediately feel like a mother, an adult.

Damien and Lila come to visit us every afternoon during our stay in the maternity ward. After they leave in the evening, I don't feel abandoned, as I did when Lila was born once Damien left my room. He would leave early, telling me he was tired of my mother always being there.

Soon we go home, our life as a foursome begins, while the hearing is fast approaching. It takes place on May 17, but I don't want to go there, I don't want to look at my mother. My lawyer will go alone.

We receive the judgment on July 2, 2009.

A psychiatric expertise is entrusted to a child psychiatrist of La Rochelle.

The grandparents are granted temporary access to the child in a neutral location on the first Saturday of each month, pending the results of the expertise.

Passages from some of Dr. Gauthier's and Dr. Carrez's letters are used in the minutes of the judgment.

I am satisfied with this psychiatric expertise. On the other hand, the right to visit, even if supervised, in a neutral place, displeases me. I go to the association that takes care of these visits. I was told that Lila would be alone with her grandparents. There will be a professional, but he will not stay in the room with them. I explain to the person who receives me that, under these circumstances, I will not present my daughter on the scheduled date, October 3.

Neither my lawyer nor my entourage approve of this decision, which is contrary to the judgment.

"If your parents file a complaint?"

I go to the gendarmerie to find out what I'm facing: a reminder of the law, for the smallest penalty; prison, for the maximum penalty. In any case, if my parents file a complaint, it will be transmitted to the prosecutor and I will be sentenced. But convicted for what?

I choose to take this risk and inform the judge in charge of the case by mail.

I have made the decision to no longer deny my past, I am becoming more free to trust my feelings. I will not let anyone stand in my way.

A DECISION THAT DOES JUSTICE

July 28, 2009
To the attention of the Family Court Judge, High Court.

I have just seen again today Mrs. Delphine Robin, whose case you are following concerning the evaluation of a right of access of her daughter by her own parents.

Some time ago, I had sent him a letter in which I did not commit myself to the particular circumstances which are his at the moment but which concerned those which generally surround the Münchhausen syndrome by proxy, which is rare and which is not always known.

She gave this letter to her lawyer but not to you, for fear of appearing too insistent.

I gave him the advice to share it with you, instead, as part of the very difficult evaluation you are facing.

I would like to inform you that Mrs Delphine Robin has sent me some rather worrying information today: among other things, her elder brother has sent her parents a letter aiming at establishing that they were reference persons to support them in their approach aiming at being able to see their grand-daughter. However this elder brother, for example, being child himself, was invited by the

*mother of Mrs Delphine Robin to take part in the blows that this
last one received from her mother on the level of the kidneys to
cause pains which she could then allege near the various doctors
concerned.*

*I cannot commit myself in this way, of course, from a distance,
and I am only reporting here the words of my patient. Nevertheless,
once again, all this seems to me to go directly in the direction of a
thorough and indispensable psychiatric evaluation of the different
people involved in this upcoming judgment.*

Doctor Carrez, psychiatrist, Nantes

It's October 3, I'm watching the hands of the clock move forward
while the kids are napping. 14 h 30. Time for Lila to meet her
grandparents. I know they are going to file a complaint for failure
to present a child. At 4:00 p.m., the phone rings. It's the gendarmerie. Although he is doing his job, the officer addresses me rather
aggressively, even though I am at fault. I simply explain to him that
I am aware of what I am doing. Nothing more. We continue our
weekend activities as normal.

The next day, a police car pulls up in front of our house. The
officer knocks on the door. I am alarmed, it is not possible, what
does he want from me? I know I didn't respect the judge's decision,
so what?

The officer tells me that he has come to apologize for being
"unpleasant" on the phone. He also tells me that he has to take
my statement following the complaint filed by my parents. He
explains to me that one of his colleagues saw my parents leaving
the premises and told him to go and consult the file on this case.

"I understand your choice, but you must still abide by the law."

A few days later, he comes to tell me the sentence that has been
imposed on me: a reminder of the law, which consists of a written
document that I must sign and which points out the acts that I have
committed against the law.

Now we just have to wait for the psychiatric expertise, which will take place on October 20th.

I am bringing all my medical records and documents regarding this procedure. This may help the doctor better understand my current decision, in case I am unable to express myself properly.

But I managed to let myself go, I put myself back in the shoes of the little girl I was, I let my emotions speak, I went back over the events I lived through, I freed myself.

On the way back, I have doubts, I am worried about what will happen next. Will this expertise be in my favor? My mother has to come by a few days later, I don't know when. I hope that she will not manage to "fool" this doctor, as she was able to do with the others, with me.

December 2009
Report of the psychiatric expertise

- To hear Lila's mother, Miss (sic) Delphine Robin.
- To hear Lila's grandmother, Mrs. Martine Robin, wife Robin.
- To determine whether grandparents can be granted access and accommodation.
- And in this hypothesis, to give its opinion on the modalities of its organization in the respect of the interest of the child.

Interview with ^{Ms.} Martine Robin

Biographical and factual information according to my interlocutor

Mrs. Martine Robin had three children, including two boys. Jerome, the elder one, "who is in drugs like Mr. Paquereau" (her daughter's husband) and "who is marginal like Mr. Robin's brother (Mrs. Martine Robin's husband)". The youngest is rather shy and reserved.

She comes from "an anxious family" and had intense fears herself despite her own mother's very protective upbringing.

Delphine "is not an accident" but a deliberately conceived child, and until the age of 4 she developed normally, then she presented urinary infections. The clinical investigations showed a bilateral reflux of the bladder contents towards the kidneys. She was treated for this and, following a traffic accident in 1990, the doctors found that she had a non-functioning kidney. "I made a big mistake in correcting a blood dosage to speed up the kidney transplant. I thought that if we put another one in, she would get better.

Her daughter's doctors diagnosed her with Munchausen's syndrome by proxy, but she disputes this because, she says, "I stopped after the transplant. (She evades the intervention of the children's judge, but her husband, heard alone after her, notes that it balanced his wife's anxieties about their daughter's condition).

Mrs. Delphine Robin has always been distressed, either by darkness or by death, and until July 15, 2008, according to Mrs. Martine Robin, she maintained a fusional relationship with her mother.

At the age of 16, her daughter met Mr. Damien Paquereau and, after a few months, they got married. In the summer of 2005, she told him that she was expecting a baby and when Lila was born, she called him to let him know. She came to see them about twice a week with Lila and although my interlocutor was very possessive of her daughter, Mrs. Delphine Robin (wife Paquereau) agreed to let them have custody of Lila, as needed, for a few half-days. When Delphine returned to work, she preferred to place her daughter in a day care center rather than entrust her to either of the grandmothers.

At Easter 2008, during a family meal, Mrs. Delphine Robin had a heated argument with her older brother, Jérôme; she insulted him in very rude terms and her older brother slapped her.

Delphine felt unsupported during this quarrel, each member present felt that she was the one who started the argument.

In July, Delphine cut off all contact with her mother and since then has refused to introduce Lila to her parents. My interlocutor's repeated approaches were met with a categorical refusal, without her being able to find out why her daughter is acting this way. Mrs. Robin and her husband consulted a lawyer who advised them to be careful. She then suggested that they see a psychologist together, but she refused. They decided to start a procedure because :

- She wonders if Delphine Robin is thinking of her daughter's welfare by removing her from her grandparents, "who are an integral part of the family nucleus. She clarifies this analysis by citing the anecdote of a chance meeting with Lila "who sent her lots of kisses and wanted to come with her.

- She is convinced that her daughter is afraid that Lila will prefer her grandmother to her and that she chose to breastfeed her "so she wouldn't have to share bottles.

- She feels that her daughter "wants to punish her by depriving her of Lila, but in doing so she is punishing Lila.

Analysis

They are postponed after the interview with Mrs. Delphine Robin.

Interview with Ms. Delphine Robin

Biographical and factual information according to my interlocutor

As soon as she sits down, she bursts into tears and apologizes for not being able to keep her resolution to control her emotions.

She recalls a jumble of memories that we will try to order chronologically. Since she was very young, she has had urinary tract infections and she has always felt that her mother was waiting for her to say that she was sick. She remembers her mother kicking her in the kidneys and her older brother doing the same. It didn't seem right to her and she complained, saying "you're not a real mother.

A decision that does justice

Before medical consultations, Mrs. Martine Robin recommended that she say that she was in pain... One day, she thinks she remembers having caught her mother and brother writing on a sheet of paper. It was afterwards that she realized that she had falsified medical results, but the doctors detected the deception. A report was made to the children's judge and a placement was considered, which worried her a lot.

She was very anxious about death because she was afraid that her remaining kidney would stop working after the "sick" kidney was removed.

Her mother had diabetes, so she also checked her blood sugar and had her hospitalized once in 1997 after these tests.

As a teenager, she met Mr. Paquereau, and when her mother learned that she had this lover, she slapped and insulted her. When her mother walked away from her, she said she had a sore back, and again, the mother's preoccupation centered on her.

When she lived with Mr. Paquereau, her mother went through a period of professional difficulties and spoke of suicide.

In 2004, Mrs. Delphine Robin went through a depressive phase and her fear of death reawakened as it had during her childhood. She consulted a psychiatrist, then a psychotherapist. It was then that she conceived Lila. Her mother was delighted, she wanted to accompany her to the ultrasounds and come to her house. She came every day despite the reluctance of Mr. Paquereau and herself.

At Easter 2008, she had a violent argument with her older brother, who slapped her. She did not understand that the whole family accused her of provoking her brother. She wanted "to get away from the maternal pressure that was suffocating her daughter, as it had happened with [her].

In July 2008, she hesitated to cut her ties and decided to take some distance. In August 2008, Mrs. Martine Robin appealed to the justice.

Mrs. Delphine Robin then undertook to reconstitute her personal history by meeting all the doctors who had treated her (she gave me a bag with three folders filled with photocopies of her medical files and we will summarize the main elements contributing to a better understanding of her care).

When Lila was born, she decided to breastfeed her "to prevent her mother from taking her in her arms". She almost separated from her husband, who could not stand Mrs. Martine Robin's constant intrusions into their family life. She was afraid that she would "turn her daughter against her" and divert her affection to herself.

On several occasions after 2008, Ms. Martine Robin tried to see Lila, for example by going to the daycare center against parental advice.

Delphine Robin tells me that she worries that her mother will pop up at any moment, and while her tone is resolute, she is not sure she can deal with it now. Access to the medical records has upset her and she sometimes fears that she will act like her mother with Lila. She holds back from taking her to the doctor for fear of repeating the same Munchausen syndrome by proxy.

Her husband advises her to go back to counseling, "but she prefers to go it alone.

Data of the complementary documents transmitted by Mrs Delphine Robin

Mrs. Delphine Robin sent me the letter she wrote to her mother and her reconstituted medical file. Her letter to her mother repeats the elements of her presentation. She evokes a sadomasochistic relationship with her mother during childhood ("at the time, I liked the mother that you were when I pleased you by saying that I was in pain") and maintained by an attachment that was both fusional and rejecting ("this vulgar way of talking to us, of getting rid of us during the summer vacations") which created a dependency ("at the beginning, I cried and I only waited for one thing, the return").

Her depression, in 2004, at the same time as Lila's conception, pushed her to look for the deep causes of her malaise. As she discovered the influence of her mother in her current psychological

A decision that does justice

suffering, she felt her mother's presence as a threat to her unborn and born daughter. Her gradual "estrangement" triggered a reinforcement of her mother's hold until the current power struggle, in which Lila is the stake.

I retained two letters from the medical record review.

Doctor Carrez notes in October 1993 that, in spite of the ablation of the kidney of her daughter, Mrs Martine Robin continues to request medical examinations for various symptoms. He proposes to the judge of the children a prolonged separation of Mrs Delphine Robin with her family, using then the term of maltreatment with child which is coupled with the diagnosis of syndrome of Münchhausen by proxy. Doctor Gauthier, associating himself with the letter of his colleague, proposes to try again "a close psychotherapeutic care of the family", but also recognizes that behind the appearance of the normality, these mothers perceive their child in a delirious way.

In an earlier letter to a colleague, Dr. Gauthier said that Delphine Robin was in danger and that the infernal circle of consultations and hospitalizations linked to maternal descriptions should be stopped. He added that Mrs Martine Robin had admitted to having manipulated the results of a large number of complementary examinations.

In October 2008, Dr. Brissaud provided Mrs. Delphine Robin with an attestation in which he described "the course of events that led to the loss of one of your kidneys as a result of additional examination manipulations".

Analysis of data from medical and psychological examinations

Mrs. Martine Robin did not reveal much about her personal life, adopting a defensive attitude in her remarks, as if the expert was mandated to judge the merits of the case and to say who is in the right. She denied being affected by Münchhausen syndrome by

proxy, "because after the transplant, she stopped her requests for examinations and consultations".

In fact, a review of the medical records belies her allegations and, until 1997, she pursued her daughter with her projective concerns about her body dysfunction.

People with this syndrome have a psyche characterized by certain psychopathological elements: the prevalence of the cleavage mechanism, an underlying depressive state with a feeling of inner emptiness and mechanisms of denial of reality that can explain the non-recognition of the continuous suffering endured by the person who is the object of this syndrome.

Mrs. Martine Robin did not, at any time, criticize the merits of her incessant medical procedures concerning her daughter. She admits a big mistake (the falsification of the creatinine dosage figures), but she absolves herself of this fault by affirming that she wanted Mrs Delphine Robin to get better. She describes psychological disorders in her daughter (anxiety about death and separation), but she does not correlate them with the painful and incessant care that she has undergone. This absence of empathy for her and of feelings of guilt is part of the psychopathological processes of cleavage (apparently normal personality, cohabiting in parallel with an irrational conception of the other's body, felt as dysfunctional).

We also recognize a denial of reality, since she claims to have ceased her medical harassment after 1991, whereas the doctors concerned referred the matter to the children's judge in 1993. Likewise, she persists in saying that she does not understand her daughter's attitude, whereas for the past year she has been able to become aware of her daughter's position, in particular during the procedure that she provoked or by reading the letters sent by her daughter.

Delphine Robin remained involved in a fusional bond with her mother until 2003-2004. She became aware that her mother had established a relationship of control with her that had made

A decision that does justice

her tutelary support and presence almost indispensable to her daily existence.

She aptly describes how this type of relational transaction makes the one who undergoes it dependent, devalued by her feelings of inferiority and by the consequences of rejections that make her doubt her value. It is her desire for a child that has been the driving force behind the critical reworking of her past:

- She first feared that the fantastical (but related to the medical reality undergone) maternal attacks had deprived her of her ability to give birth, and then to carry out this pregnancy.

- At birth, Lila became a precious "object" that she feared her mother would steal from her, either by disqualifying her as a mother ("she loves her grandmother more than me") or by exerting a hold on the little girl.

By including the grandparents in the family nucleus and by validating her daughter's rivalry with her, by her comments on Lila's breastfeeding to prevent her from giving the bottle or on her daughter's fear of being less loved, Mrs. Martine Robin, once again, maintains Mrs. Delphine Robin's anguish and resolutely pursues her relationship of hold and control over her. The speed with which she went to court shows that this power relationship is the driving force behind her bond with Ms. Delphine Robin and that Lila is the stake in it.

It implicitly implies that the latter is, as previously the body of Mrs. Delphine Robin, under her influence and that she can dispose of it as she wants.

Ms. Delphine Robin deciphered the message that she does not own Lila and cannot take her away from her maternal grandmother.

The doctors had recommended the separation of Mrs. Delphine Robin with her family because they knew that this long-term measure could allow first the defusion, then the reconstruction associated with a psychotherapeutic work. This measure was not retained and, in fact, Mrs Delphine Robin remained under the influence of her mother.

At present, Mrs. Delphine Robin is trying to apply this rupture in order to get out of the rut in which she is involved in the relationship with her mother (and in which she fears to drag her daughter). Lila should not be an obstacle to this personal and couple process, because I have perceived how much Mrs. Delphine Robin needs to feel that she is free of the external hold in order to tackle, through psychotherapy, her internal disarray.

If we recognize that Münchhausen syndrome by proxy is child abuse (and by saying this we are not stigmatizing Mrs. Martine Robin in the effect of her disorders on her daughter), it is appropriate to support Mrs. Delphine Robin's current request to be able to stabilize herself, to secure herself, to restructure herself psychologically out of her family's influence and thus to be able to try to avoid dragging Lila into this family conflict.

She will not be able to "cope alone" and must consider personal psychotherapy and parenting guidance (with her husband), in order to free the education she gives to Lila from the repetitions of the past and the attitudes of defense against them.

Martine Robin should have recognized the suffering inflicted on her daughter and eventually entered into family therapy in order to establish other links between the various family members. This approach would be ineffective at present, because it would appear to be a manipulative form of appeasement of the conflict with her daughter in order to maintain her bond of control. The precipitous court action has revealed the stakes it places on Lila and it would be unwise to grant her request in its current configuration.

I want to let everyone know. He believed me, he believed me! He understood! I can't believe it! Thanks to this doctor, the judge will give me the right to freedom, my long journey will be supported by justice!

I am sending a copy of this psychiatric report to the doctors who supported me - Dr. Hacquin, Dr. Florent, Dr. Gauthier, Dr. Carrez and Professor Brissaud.

The court decision will be rendered on November 4, 2010: "The child's interest is to live in a peaceful circle of people, which seems possible in the present state only by restricting the family unit to the girl and her parents."

Conclusion

For three years, until September 2012, I will work every Monday with a psychotherapist recommended by Dr. Carrez, Mrs. Aline. I become aware of my painful repressed childhood history thanks to the awakening of my emotions. My therapist does not give any personal opinion, does not find any argument that would make me guilty of what I have lived. This is what I did for a long time. I appreciate coming to confide in her without being judged. I found the right therapist.

As the weeks and months go by, the anxious, fearful little girl begins to disappear from my thoughts. Sometimes I find myself curled up in bed at night and crying. I end up falling asleep, I wake up a little later, my kidney hurts. Sore? I also find the pain I felt when my father was giving me shots in my buttocks to treat my urinary tract infections. I understand that through these physical sensations, I am taking ownership of my history. To relive, to feel, to understand, to accept, this is the price to pay to free myself.

I am beginning to stop blaming myself, to stop feeling guilty, I can develop empathy for the child who has suffered from the behavior of his mother and the medical world. I suffered and buried my anger. A latent hatred accompanied me for many years and triggered various symptoms in my body, a malaise. Today, I can consciously feel my revolt against my mother's manipulations that made me suffer and that I was asked to forget.

Today, I know what price I had to pay for what is called "resilience".

I am on a journey to take control of my life and to do whatever I feel is necessary to rebuild my mind and body.

I cancel my "100% long term illness" coverage. I don't want it to appear on my Vitale card anymore, I am not sick! I get my new certificate in two months.

I also decided to finally get rid of my scar that has been bothering me for so many years and that is a physical stigma of what I have been through. Luckily, I did not have to face a new general anesthesia.

At work, I asked to change departments to work in an office: after Victor's birth, every day in geriatrics was hell and brought me back to my childhood suffering. The weakness of the elderly, their inability to express their anger, their submission were intolerable. Every morning I had a lump in my stomach, I was drained of all the tears that my body had held back in the evening. I don't repress my emotions anymore, but I don't want to wear myself out fighting for the cause of others, a cause for which, moreover, I am not understood.

The biggest job was with Lila.

It took many sessions for Mrs. Aline to get me to verbalize and accept my relationship difficulties with my daughter. The relationship with the mother I am afraid that Lila will drag me into an intense relationship.

Our relationship becomes invasive for me and insecure for Lila. The more I feel this intensity between us, the more I detach myself from her. She feels this distance and, as a result, "clings" to me even more. Separation frightens her, life in the community is more or less complicated for her ("Lila doesn't play, Lila stays glued to an adult"). I would like her to play, I would like her to enjoy going to the others, I would like her to appreciate when we have to leave each other. But no, she holds me back when she feels the separation coming and I get angry, I panic. When she finally falls asleep at night, after having asked me ten times, I isolate myself to cry. This makes the daily life of the four of us extremely difficult.

Telling Lila the truth. That's what I need to do. Tell her openly about the difficult relationship between me and her grandmother and how it has affected my life as an adult and as a mother. Give up denying my suffering, develop empathy for the child I was.

I sought help from a child psychiatrist. Lila didn't really agree. The consultations were difficult for me, I couldn't hold back my emotions and I cried a little. Lila was silent. She would only respond with nods of the head. But she listened, she heard the difficulties I expressed to the doctor.

We went there three times. It may not seem like much, but the change is obvious. Bedtime is going better. She still tries to hold me back a bit, but she only calls me back once to tuck her in again. She doesn't wake up at night anymore, whereas she used to come to our room several times, anxious. At school, at daycare, at the dance, she doesn't hold on to me anymore.

All these small changes are a huge step forward. I feel more relaxed, I'm not afraid of being swallowed up anymore.

To think that the first days of Lila's life, I was the one who "smothered" her, for fear that my mother would steal my daughter, I understand that it is confusing for her now. It is up to me to reassure her, while reassuring myself. Lila read in my eyes the insecure and lost mother that I was and against whom I fight for my well-being and hers.

Nevertheless, it was necessary to consult a psychoanalyst again, as Lila's behavior was becoming worrisome again as a result of her grandmother's repeated and regular incursions after her class, and especially after she entered the playground to introduce herself to her granddaughter. This psychoanalyst, whom Lila had seen seven times, was able to explain to her my particular history with my mother.

Conclusion

Now I feel that Lila is lighter, free of a weight. The questions she had have been asking herself have been answered, she understands better and she talks about this delicate situation more easily.

In time, my hatred for my mother may diminish and even disappear. Life events may suddenly bring back certain memories, but now I know what they are. I know myself well enough because I have experienced again the feelings of the little girl I once was, and the last trace of guilt in me has disappeared. I have admitted the truth, overcome my fears and am no longer afraid to reveal who my mother really was, what my story was.

I would like, one day, to be able, in all modesty, to change the way the general public sees things. I have no doubt that my emotional honesty will one day be able to break down the wall of ignorance that surrounds the repression of the child tormented by the abuse he or she suffers and that will continue until adulthood if no one helps.

"Abuse." I still find it difficult to pronounce this word. But yes, the Münchhausen syndrome by proxy is indeed a form of mistreatment, under its cuddly appearances.

But today, thanks to the help of my witnesses, Professor Brissaud, Dr. Carrez and Dr. Gauthier, and thanks to my own willpower, I live with a zest for life that I would not want to lose for anything in the world!

ACKNOWLEDGEMENTS

Thank you to all the doctors who agreed to meet me, so many years later.

Thank you for supporting me in the procedure that my mother and parents imposed on me.

Thanks to justice.

A big thank you to Dr. Lecourt, this doctor who saw my mother and me only once, but who understood remarkably well my mother's particular personality, and what was essential for me, for the well-being of my family.

A special thank you to Professor Brissaud, I remain convinced that he was the most important person in this story, he knew how to unmask my mother's manipulations, to protect the little girl that I was.

Thanks also to Dr. Gauthier and Dr. Carrez who had a very important role in this story.

Thank you to Mrs. Aline, who is my psychotherapist.

This story, as dramatic as it may have been, made me the person I am today.

In order to live, the child has no other solution than to ignore his suffering in order to privilege the illusion of being loved and of loving his parent.

AFTERWORD

Having defended my medical thesis on Munchausen's syndrome by proxy in 2001, I gladly accepted the author's request to write this afterword because it is essential to support the victims of such abuse.

Reading the whole book in one go brings many emotions: stupefaction and fascination constantly renewed in front of the unfolding drama (appearance of the maternal lies and then of the falsifications of the complementary examinations, physical violence), identification with the pain, the sadness and the anger of the author as a child and as an adult, anxious expectation of a positive outcome and finally joy of the final relief in noting the care lavished on Mrs. Paquereau and the early preventive measures for her children. I am questioned from the very first chapters by the place of the brother, then by the exercise of memory with its selectivity and the confrontation with past pain. The author has an authentic style to put herself in the place of the little girl she was. In the first part, the reader sees the relationship of control being established and the abuse being installed in her relationship with the medical world. The contrast between the girl's feelings and the content of the medical letters is striking. During the reading of the book, the existential questions of the selectivity of the memory and the primordial need of affection (attachment) between the parent (here the mother) and the child are raised to the detriment of the pathology. Everything happens as if it were better "to be together and sick" than "separated and without disease". Depressive elements appear when the mother-daughter bond begins to be less fusional in 2004. The effects of repression in the adult girl and denial in the abusive mother are powerful; the exploitation of the child's love by the abusive mother works until the author's second pregnancy is discovered. The attention the mother seeks and receives is also well described, both medical and non-medical.

The effects of lying remain fascinating and the question of being believed or not being believed persists beyond the symptoms, beyond adulthood. This reinforced my motivation to participate and to detail the existence of this little-known pathology. The point of view of the child's experience (now adult) is rarely heard or studied in the medical literature on this syndrome. Antoine de Saint-Exupéry said that "one is of one's childhood as one is of one's country"; how can one keep one's identity and how can one build oneself according to one's surroundings when one's childhood is filled with the thoughts and actions of a bad mother? I have a lot of admiration for Ms. Paquereau for finally being able to express what the granddaughter-in-her-face felt and a lot of gratitude because she shares it with us. May this book contribute to help Delphine Paquereau and all the child victims to find their way to reparation!

Some theoretical elements concerning this pathology

Munchausen syndrome by proxy (MMPP) is located at the border of the pediatric, psychiatric and legal fields. Described since 1977 by Meadow, this extreme form of child abuse involves a mother inducing symptoms in her child that she brings before the medical profession for diagnostic and therapeutic explorations at the expense of the child. She manipulates the clinical history and produces physical symptoms and/or abnormal complementary results, in order to obtain consistent medical attention. Confusion, lack of awareness of this syndrome and difficulty in making the diagnosis are the reasons for its underestimated frequency and potential seriousness (mortality of at least 7%, heavy legal implications). The enigmatic psychopathology of SMPP highlights the confusion and fascination of these triangular mother-child-physician relationships.

The most pragmatic current definition of SMPP is proposed by Rosenberg in 1987 based on the following four diagnostic criteria: 1) illness in a child, simulated and/or produced by one of the two parents; 2) repeated presentation of the child for medical or surgical care leading to multiple diagnostic and therapeutic procedures; 3) denial of knowledge of the illness by the responsible parent; 4) regression of symptoms when parent-child separation is instituted

The epidemiology of SMPP shows a so-called exceptional frequency (250 cases documented from 1977 to 2001). The perpetrator of the factitious disorders is the child's natural mother in 95% of cases; her average age at the time of diagnosis is 29 years; these mothers are over-represented in the paramedical professions, have a personal history of factitious disorders and are socially, emotionally and family isolated. The victim of factitious disorders is of indifferent sex (as many girls as boys), the average age at diagnosis is 3 years and 4 months; the average delay in making the diagnosis is 14 months; it is most often the last child of the siblings.

The symptoms combine a *pseudologica fantastica* (extraordinary and flamboyant lies in the form of imprecise and impressive mythomaniacal discourse marking the anamnesis in the image of the *Extraordinary Adventures of Baron Münchhausen*) and factitious disorders of three possible kinds: invented, simulated and provoked.

In his 1987 literature review of 117 cases of SMPP, Rosenberg lists the methods of fabricating the factitious disorders of SMPP and finds:

- 25% of cases of false claims without active production. The symptoms can be classified into two categories: isolated false claims (examples: comitiveness, apnea, vomiting, asthma) and falsification of complementary examinations (examples: hemorrhagic manifestations, fever, high blood pressure, urinary lithiasis).

- 25% multi-symptomatic false claims with and without active production.

- 50% of cases of false claims with active production. These symptoms often need to be seen by the physician (examples: bleeding manifestations, comitiality, central nervous system depression, apnea, diarrhea, vomiting, fever, skin rash or inflammation, asthma, urinary lithiasis).

Isolated allegations by the mother, without any actual acting out on her part, have the same consequences for the child and the medical relationship.

The behaviour combines "hospital wandering", a tendency for the child to agree with the parent and a particular attitude during care: a fusional mother-child relationship, an attitude of "perfect mother", an attitude of anxiety and a feeling of injustice, and then denial of the facts as soon as the slightest suspicion is raised against her. Four categories of behaviour are distinguished: "doctor addicts", "help-seekers", "active inducers" and "*active* neglects". As far as the "*active* inducers" are concerned, this form is the most characteristic of the SMPP inducers, and also the one that is diagnosed the latest because of the intensity of the deception. The mother appears to be good beyond suspicion and the child is often an infant or preschooler. The mother directly causes symptoms on the child that put his health and his life in danger. The symptoms are diverse and dramatic. They are characterized by extreme denial with projection and dissociation of affects. The confrontation with the truth can lead to suicidal action. The literature provides very few detailed descriptions of the diagnosis or the dynamics of these mothers, as they are notoriously resistant to any treatment and flee from any therapeutic intervention.

Psychopathology finds a disruption of doctor-patient relationships with indirect presentation of symptoms through the child. The mothers are trusting and compliant in the care of the child. There is a pleasure in abuse and deception, masochistic personality traits and an autoerotic dimension in the performance of aggressive behaviors.

Meadow was the first to develop a list of warning signs that should prompt vigilance; his list has been expanded by other authors such as Rosenberg. However, these warning signs are difficult to use as a guide for physicians. "Just thinking about it" is not an easy method. Indeed, one must rely on the characteristics of a particular relationship to the medical world that includes denial. It seems that many of these situations are unrecognized (hence the "recent discovery" of this pathology of the mother-child bond).

We can therefore consider to be in the presence of elements of suspicion when the child's illness presents several facets: it is long, persistent or recurrent, unusual or even rare, appearing as a unique case; when the symptoms and clinical signs have no semiological link between them, they are inappropriate, incongruous, unusual; when there is an extreme discordance between the clinical signs observed, the normality of the paraclinical examinations and the general state of the child very often preserved; when the symptoms are particularly alarming (examples: comitial seizures observed only by the mother and not responding to anti-comitial treatments, polymicrobial bacteremia with incompatible germs); when the signs and symptoms disappear in the mother's absence; when the father is always absent during the child's hospitalization; when the mother says she does not know the cause of the illness (denial); when the mother shows excessive attachment to the child and remains constantly at the child's bedside; when the mother maintains friendly relations with the hospital staff: described as a model mother, she seeks to be involved in the care of other children and to comfort the nursing staff, she appears closer to the nursing staff than actually present with her child (most often she shows great confidence and compliance with the nursing service while the caregivers do not have this serenity; more rarely she shows dissatisfaction, recrimination, or even aggression); When the mother appears intelligent: When the mother gives the impression of being less concerned than the doctor: she welcomes all medical explorations performed on the child, even when the investigation procedures prove to be painful for the child; When there is a history of sudden infant death syndrome within the same sibling; When the child has numerous allergies; When the child does not tolerate the treatment well: vomiting is frequent, as well as skin inflammation and problems due to the infusions

Various factors contribute to the obstacle of the diagnosis

Medical "blindness" remains the primary explanation for missed diagnoses, due to the lack of knowledge of the syndrome in medical circles, especially in places far from university hospitals. Nevertheless, this tendency is less marked since we have witnessed in the last few years a certain craze for this fascinating pathology.

The non-recognition of the diagnosis is illustrated by the estimated average delay of fourteen months between the first fake signs and the diagnosis. First the doctor starts by "believing the mother's convinced and convincing denial", then the unsuccessful search for the origin of the symptoms will reinforce the doctor's zeal with repeated hospitalizations. For the doctor, who is neither a judge nor a detective, accepting the diagnosis of SMPP means recognizing that he has been trapped in his knowledge and power. What the mother is looking for is precisely to destroy the common illusion of the patient's trusting and passive submission to the medical omnipotence. She attacks the Master's word by showing two things: that he is mistaken (therefore impotent) and that he is dangerous. By making him alienated from his position of all-knowing, it attacks the doctor on a narcissistic and imaginary level so that he can no longer recognize his error.

The physician and nursing staff are convinced of the mother's attachment to the child as opposed to a suspicious attitude. The pediatric staff is keen to create positive interactions with the parents (hence the unrestricted visitation for parents and also the mother-child hospitalizations). Thus, the "fusional" mother-child relationship elicits discretion and withdrawal on the part of caregivers who oppose a diagnostic possibility. Separation anxiety and hyperprotection are not expected in situations of abuse.

Finally, to avoid being found out, the mother moves or changes doctors or hospitals. If she is discovered, she always denies it. The development of computerized systems (carte vitale), which are in conflict with the infringement of individual freedom, has not yet made it possible to collate the opinions of different doctors on the same child (hospital vagrancy), nor to allow for follow-up in order to prevent recidivism.

Convincing the courts of the reality of this syndrome is a real difficulty, especially in England and the United States, where the theme of the absence of proof of abuse is recurrent. The lack of knowledge of SMPP by judges and other legal professionals also prevents the rapid adoption of protective measures for the child, including separation from the mother if necessary.

The limits are sometimes thin with the normality of stressed parents and, given the difficulty of proving the diagnosis, one must count on a probably important undiagnosed non-diagnosis (frequent suspicion in general medicine as in pediatrics).

Medical prognosis is an aspect that has been little studied in the literature, apart from mortality. According to the studies, mortality varies from 7 to 10%, so this is a major statistical fact that should be kept in mind by all professionals. The main risk factor seems to be certain symptomatic forms of factitious disorders: the main causes of death are manual asphyxia and intoxication with psychotropic drugs, water or salt.

The short-term morbidity rate is 100%. This refers to painful symptoms inflicted and experienced by the child, and resolved without permanent deformity or functional deficit. The more invasive the medical intervention (complementary examinations, medical or surgical treatments) (surgery, central catheterization, arteriography, etc.), the worse the prognosis.

Long-term morbidity refers to symptoms resulting in permanent deformity or functional impairment. The physical morbidity is evaluated between 8 and 10% of cases according to the authors. This means that in 90% of cases no permanent physical sequelae have been identified. These sequelae depend on the type of symptom induced. They are mainly surgical sequelae after multiple interventions on the digestive tract, neurological sequelae with central paralysis, cortical blindness and/or mental retardation, joint lesions with lameness and transmission of the HIV virus by transfusion. Many multioperated patients of the abdomen (laparotomy, colectomy or ileostomy) are predisposed to subsequent complications.

Psychological morbidity has been little studied. It is part of a broader context of comorbidity than SMPP. It is not just a consequence of physical morbidity. Infants often have eating disorders. Preschoolers are often socially withdrawn, hyperactive and oppositional. These children often show preoccupation with their bodily integrity (fear of being sick) or feel threatened (fear of being poisoned or dying). At school age, there is sometimes a picture of "chronic invalidism" with marked separation anxieties. They seem to learn quickly to passively tolerate medical procedures. Restrictive measures imposed by their mothers (dietary restrictions, strict living conditions, limitation of social contacts) and school absenteeism due to hospitalizations exclude and marginalize the child relatively early. Older children sometimes have conversion symptoms and may cooperate with parental deception. In adulthood, behavioral or personality disorders develop with immaturity, emotional instability, intolerance to constraints and ease of acting out. Finally, sometimes the syndrome appears to be transgenerational; the child victim of SMPP will suffer from SM in adulthood, just as the perpetrator of SMPP has a history of SM in childhood.

Regarding sibling morbidity, Hatier cites 11% of siblings who died at an early age of unexplained causes, 39% who were victims of SMPP and 17% who were victims of physical abuse or neglect. These figures are very disturbing since the 11% who died at a young age are clearly above the norms of the general population: statistically, they are homicides. It is therefore of the utmost importance that for each suspicion of SMPP a systematic investigation of the siblings be carried out. The extension of an SMPP to the siblings would be correlated to the existence of serious personality disorders in the mother. Thus, the risk of extension of SMPP to the siblings, estimated by the authors to be between 9 and 25% of cases, should also influence the management of the child and his or her siblings. The child victim of SMPP is most often the youngest of the siblings, the mother transferring to the youngest child a behavior by proxy that she induced before in the previous child.

And the child in all this?

The SMPP focuses attention on the mother. There is little research on the psychopathology of the child victim. The child's psyche, ignored primarily by the mother, seems to be ignored by practitioners. Any child (and all the more so the younger he or she is) seems likely to be a victim of a SMPP, which perhaps explains in part the fascination that surrounds this syndrome despite its extreme rarity. Indeed, the absolute dependence in the first phases of life on the omnipotence of the mother sends everyone back to the imaginary child victim that he or she might have been. By offering an ideal model of a guilty mother, the monstrous spectre of the SMPP-inducing mother allows one to exorcise one's own infantile anguish linked to the dependence on the omnipotence of one's mother.

The SMPP refers, as far as the child victim is concerned, to the notion of ideal support with the "sufficiently good mother" (according to D. Winnicott): here the mother is "too good" because she is too anticipatory, mastering everything and alone knowing the answers to the riddles she raises. This maternal behavior is frequently underpinned by a maternal depression that hinders the child's autonomy process. It is a pervasive system of disabling. The child is aware that it is not the mother's fault and that she is there to support him... By projective identification, the mother, refusing to mentalize the ambivalence of any mother-child relationship, experiences the child and her thinking as a threat. It is there that is all the psychological morbidity of the child who is not any more subject but controlled object; seduced and accomplice, in situation of hold, the child slips towards the alienation under the hold of its bodily pathology (extension of the maternal body) and bends under the posted love of this "exemplary mother". The child cannot resort to the father who sees nothing. Independence is not possible for the child under the yoke of passivity and assuetude. Only the symbolic instance of the Law can help the father to take back his place during the diagnosis of the SMPP.

The child lives in a morbid paradox: "to be alone is impossible" because the child is the guardian of the maternal psychic integrity and "to be together is obligatory but dangerous" because the sacrificed child is the object of control by expiatory delegation of the faults committed by the mother's own parents.

The child is thus in the role of mediator of maternal intrapsychic conflicts thanks to the delegation (proxy). Their relations are of symbiotic type; he is invaded by the mother of whom he is an accomplice in the collusion of the denial, in the repression of his expression even in his own capacities of representation. In the SMPP, not only does the mother impose a ban on autonomy (dependence always signified by symptoms and care) but she perverts the desire for autonomy by the confusion she induces (a false relationship with the doctor from the outset since the mother retains control of the symptoms).

About abuse

I agree with Delphine Paquereau that the care of abused children is quite poor in France and that SMPP is a very complex form of abuse. It is important to underline the really poor care to protect the child. The psychological damage to the child exists ipso facto for any type of abuse. Indeed, in case of abuse, the fundamental trauma that the child undergoes on an emotional level is that of a betrayal by the people in whom he should have total confidence, betrayal coupled with a feeling of powerlessness and negative perception of himself. Thus, apart from the fear and pain, what gives the episode its traumatic dimension is the feeling that an adult has betrayed the child's trust and affection in the absence of protection (support) by another adult. For the child, the question arises of not being loved by his parents: is this possible? Can the mother, who is his first object of love, not love him? They adhere to what their parents say and do because they think they cannot be loved in any other way or not at all. He can even idealize an abusive parent, so vital is it to him to maintain this trusting love somewhere. One cannot state the unthinkable, hence the denial (unconscious refusal).

The consequences on health are disastrous (100% morbidity), leading to serious repercussions, perpetual questions on parenthood, education and good treatment, etc. In the case of a successful awareness like that of Mrs. Paquereau, there remains a feeling of guilt which Mrs. Paquereau emphasizes the importance of getting rid of as much as possible in order to *build a lasting resilience.*

May this book help doctors and health professionals to better identify these (seemingly too perfect) mothers in order to better protect the children. As for the question of how to deal with abusive mothers, is it possible once the damage is done? Prevention towards the victimized generation remains the main way to avoid further suffering.

Dr. Stéphanie Dauver, child psychiatrist

Table of contents

Best sellers Max Milo Editions

Hitler's banker, Jean-François Bouchard

Confessions of a forger, Éric Piedoie Le Tiec

The Koran and the flesh, Ludovic-Mohamed Zahed

Governing by fake news, Jacques Baud

Governing by chaos, Collectif

A political history of food, Paul Ariès

Mad in U.S.A.: The ravages of the "American model",
Michel Desmurget

Mondial soccer club geopolitics, Kévin Veyssière

Putin: Game master?, Jacques Braud

Treatise on the three impostors: Moses, Jesus, Muhammad,
The Spirit of Spinoza

TV Lobotomy, Michel Desmurget

www.ingramcontent.com/pod-product-compliance
Lightning Source LLC
LaVergne TN
LVHW010212060726
842525LV00014B/3295